GREAT
ENGLISH
HOUSES

The Stone Hall, Houghton, an exact cube in shape. Rysbrack carved the reliefs and the bust of Sir Robert Walpole over the fireplace, as well as the doorways.

GREAT ENGLISH HOUSES

RUSSELL CHAMBERLIN

HARMONY BOOKS

NEW YORK

Published in the United States in 1983 by Harmony Books, a
division of Crown Publishers, Inc, One Park Avenue, New York,
New York 10016. HARMONY and colophon are trademarks of
Crown Publishers, Inc.

First published in 1983 in Great Britain by George Weidenfeld
and Nicolson Limited, 91 Clapham High Street, London sw4
7TA, in association with The English Tourist Board.

Printed in Italy

Library of Congress Cataloging in Publication Data
Chamberlin, E. R. (Eric Russell), 1926–
    Great English houses.

    Includes index.
    1. Architecture, Domestic—England.   2. Castles—
England.   3. Towers—England.   I. Title.
NA7328.C443   1983   728.8′0942   83–8598
ISBN 0–517–55086–5

CONTENTS

CONTENTS

THE SEVENTEENTH CENTURY

THE EIGHTEENTH CENTURY

THE NINETEENTH CENTURY

THE TWENTIETH CENTURY

Bamburgh Castle

Callaly Castle

Alnwick Castle

Meldon Park

Seaton Delaval

Raby Castle

Muncaster Castle

Constable Burton

Norton Conyers

Sutton Park

Ripley Castle

Burton Constable

Chatsworth

Hardwick Hall

Little Moreton Hall

Haddon Hall

Belvoir Castle

Holkham Hall

Burghley House

Houghton Hall

Blickling Hall

Stokesay Castle

Deene Park

Broughton Castle

Woburn Abbey

Layer Marney Tower

Eastnor Castle

Blenheim Palace

Gorhambury House

Hatfield House

Cliveden House

Hughenden Manor

Berkeley Castle

Mapledurham House

Sutton Place

Clandon Park

Knole

Ightham Mote

Longleat House

Wilton House

Loseley House

Hever Castle

Great Dixter

Purse Caundle Manor

Beaulieu Palace House

Petworth House

Penshurst Place

Arundel Castle

Castle Drogo

St Michael's Mount

A Nobleman's Levee, c. *1730*, by Marcellus Laroon, a revealing appraisal of the role of the great English house at its apogee.

INTRODUCTION

ABOUT the year 1730 Marcellus Laroon, a not otherwise particularly distinguished artist, painted a picture – *A Nobleman's Levee* – which exactly summed up the role of the great house at its apogee. In the mid-ground the nobleman, coldly indifferent to the press of petitioners awaiting him, is leisurely putting the finishing touches to his attire. On the walls in the background is evidence of his family's lineage, wealth and power in the form of portraits, paintings and tapestries. The faces and characters of those awaiting his lordship's pleasure are all strongly individual. In the left foreground an elderly gentleman, swelling with indignation at his cavalier treatment, is being calmed by a flunkey. Next to him a young fop, accustomed to being kept waiting, is offering snuff to a fellow sufferer. Beside them, a swaggering braggadocio is glaring across at the cause of their humiliation. Resignation, or anger are the predominant reactions to their indifferent reception. What Laroon has presented us with is an exact, though singularly unattractive view of life: the great house, after it had ceased to be a fortress, became a reservoir of wealth, and in order to allow that wealth to be redistributed throughout society, it was necessary to engage the attention, and the goodwill, of its owner.

Currently, each of the handsome guidebooks to Woburn, Longleat and Beaulieu – leaders in the 'stately homes industry' – bears a personal message from the house's owner. Each message is a variant on the theme that, without the public, the house could not continue to exist in its traditional form, if at all. At Longleat, the Marquess of Bath records: 'In these days of heavy taxation it would be impossible to maintain [the house] in the condition in which you see it but for your contributions.' At Beaulieu: 'Your visit helps to preserve a vital part of our national heritage.' At Woburn, the Marquess of Tavistock says unequivocally: 'We have become custodians, no longer the owners.'

The difference between the subject of Laroon's painting and these sentiments, the shift in emphasis from the crowd appealing to the single figure, to the single figure appealing to the crowd, measures the scale of the enormous, though bloodless revolution that has taken place in the interim in the United Kingdom. Until the 1880s, the majority of those who did not live in one of the chartered towns or cities, lived on one of the estates of the nobility contributing, willy-nilly, to the upkeep of the great house that formed the ganglion. The introduction of estate duty in 1894, coupled with the agricultural depression, began the great change. It accelerated in the between-war years (it has been calculated that about a quarter of the land changed hands between 1918 and 1922) and again immediately after World War II. On an estate of £1 million, some four-fifths could be demanded in death duties, unless the family successfully exploited a macabre guessing game. Duties could be avoided if the estate was passed over to the heir a fixed period (currently five years) before the death of the donor. In 1946, the Duke of Devonshire unexpectedly died just four months before the period expired, and the estate was taxed at eighty per cent. One arm of the government frequently defeats the intention of the other. In 1983, at a time when official concern was being expressed at the break-up of art collections, Customs and Excise threatened to levy Value Added Tax on the proposed 'sale' of Kedlestone Hall to the nation for a nominal £2 million, arguing that the contents were being used to attract a fee-paying public.

The ambivalent manner in which the British regard this segment of their national heritage is well illustrated by the fact that they have no adequate name for this class of building, unlike their continental equivalents – 'schloss', 'palazzo', or 'château'. The term 'country house' manages at once to be imprecise and misleading: imprecise, because any rurally situated house must obviously be a country house; misleading, because it conveys a limited, Victorian atmosphere of expensive cigars, leather upholstery and political intrigue. The currently fashionable term 'stately home', derived from Noel Coward's satirical ballad, has an air of wry self-mockery – partly envious – that faithfully reflects a period of social fragmentation and unease. 'Great house' as used in this book, has obvious limitations, but it does convey both the sense of relative size (the phrase 'the big house' is still used in rural communities when referring to the building that was once the centre of social activity) and the sense of history that imbues these houses.

The vague terminology applied to the class of house contrasts with the precise description of the

Chatsworth – the epitome of a great English country house.

house itself, which also places it at some point in history. 'Palace' is rare – very rare apart from royal and episcopal buildings. 'Castle' is a survival from the Middle Ages: Arundel, Berkeley and Alnwick are all genuinely military structures which have, almost absent-mindedly, become homes. 'Manor' describes a once vital function – the great house as a generator and reservoir of rural wealth; it was only later, in the eighteenth century, that its role as a consumer and dispenser of wealth dominated its other functions. 'Hall' is simply the description of a form or structure – the barn-like building which once served as a kind of tribal meeting place, then became a nucleus and finally a fossil. 'Abbey' or 'Priory' indicates the great plunder of the sixteenth century that accompanied the dissolution of the monasteries. 'House', like the non-use of 'palace', marks that prudent English tendency to play down possession so that the rich man will use the same term for his vast mansion as the poor man uses for his hovel. Many a manor house has upgraded itself to castle status (Stokesay and Broughton are cases in point) and many a castle is a nineteenth-century confection. But the labels do serve to give some historical orientation.

England had established its basic unit, the manor, long before the Norman Conquest, giving William an easy means to reward his followers. Each manor could have only one lord, but a lord could have many manors. In the two centuries following the Conquest, the great house was either a castle, or a defended farmhouse. The owners of these farmhouses did not automatically fortify them: permission had to be sought from the monarch, who granted his licence only reluctantly, for each fortified building created a potential threat.

From the mid-thirteenth century, another role was added to the traditional functions of defence, and agricultural production and storage: the more wealthy owners began to treat their uncompromising structures as potential homes, and indulged in a little cautious decorating. The major advance, for the very wealthy, was the use of glass in windows, following the example of such magnates as Sir Walter Poultney, who inserted glass in the walls of Penshurst in 1340.

The Great Hall continued as the centre of all social life. The floor was commonly of beaten earth strewn with rushes and known, significantly, as the marsh. Even as late as the sixteenth century the fastidious Dutchman, Erasmus, described with dis-

gust just what lay under the top layer of fresh rushes. At one end of the hall a screen cut off the entrance door and service quarters. The innately conservative English were to retain this screen long after the domestic arrangements had become more sophisticated, turning it into elaborately decorated stonework. At the other end of the hall was the raised dais for the master and his family.

The Battle of Bosworth in 1485, which brought the Wars of the Roses to an end, marked a moment of change in British history as precise as that of the Norman Conquest. The heroic period now lay in the past: the future would lie with statesmen, merchants and financiers rather than with soldiers. The new king, Henry VII, summed up the qualities of the new age in his own person – an avaricious, parsimonious man but also one imaginative enough to finance Cabot's explorations. The coming men resembled their monarch and suddenly a swarm of new families – Cavendish, Cecil, Russell, Thynne – were pushing aside the old nobility, making their fortunes through a skilful combination of commerce and political astuteness. And they began to build new houses, not simply adapting the old.

Glass windows now became a characteristic of the new type of house, evidence not only of private wealth but also the social stability that permitted domestic life to be carried out behind so frail a barrier. Battlements and gatehouses continued to be built, but as much from tradition as from necessity. The Great Hall sank in status, the family moving to more private but splendid rooms on the first floor. The introduction of flues to relieve smoke-filled rooms produced the towering fireplaces and the fantastic chimneys of Tudor England.

Architecture faithfully reflected the social changes of the mid-seventeenth century. The great Elizabethan and Jacobean mansions like Hardwick, Burghley and Knole, were by then old fashioned, though built less than a generation earlier by wealthy men and women to entertain and impress their monarch. Now rising prices, less capital and the emergence of a new middle class led imperceptibly to the building of less ostentatious houses, compensating for their loss of size with an increased opulence in interior decoration. Grinling Gibbons was among those craftsmen who gained fame and a modest fortune from this new emphasis. Confidence and arrogance came back with a flourish in the eighteenth century. The Enclosure Acts and West Indian sugar vastly increased the income of the country gentry at a time when it was fashionable to have aesthetic tastes. The injection of wealth not only resulted in a wave of rebuilding by the gentry, the medieval and Tudor houses of their ancestors making way for the latest style of brick boxes, but it also created a kind of megalomania where the greater the acreage tamed and covered, the more esteemed the architect and patron. The park now came into its own, and the names of gardeners like Capability Brown and Humphrey Repton rivalled those of architects.

Coincident with the rise of landscape gardening, 'stately home' visiting began on a large scale, unwittingly providing one of the means which was to allow the house to survive in the unimaginable twentieth century. The aristocracy had always expected, as a matter of course, to receive the hospitality of their equals while travelling, but now permission to enter and view almost any great house became widely available. Indeed, in 1778 William

Constable actually advertized that his splendidly refurbished house of Burton Constable was now open to the public, perhaps the first example of a now almost universal custom.

Uncritical admirers of the English country house are fond of claiming it as the supreme example of British architectural genius, ignoring such superb urban creations as the inns, cathedrals, guildhalls and assembly rooms which this rurally-orientated people have created. But the eighteenth century also succeeded in reducing far too many houses to a boring uniformity. Endless Red Drawing Rooms, Green Sitting Rooms and Bronze Dining Rooms took the place of chunky, differentiated, medieval and Tudor chambers. And the dreaded names of Capability Brown and Humphrey Repton, superb artists though they were, feature again and again as they dragoon the English landscape into a preconceived pattern of harmony. It is with a sense of relief and refreshment that the visitor comes to a place like

Gheeraerts' painting of Lady Sidney and her children, c. 1595, at Penshurst Place

Haddon Hall, Penshurst Place or Ightham Mote, all of which escaped that homogenizing blight and bear the marks of their centuries upon them.

It must be admitted, too, that many of the artefacts in the houses would be better displayed in a modern gallery or museum. At Knole, for instance, Reynolds' portraits of Samuel Johnson and Oliver Goldsmith are at a height and angle that makes it virtually impossible to study them. But they are placed there because that is where they were hung by the owner a year, a decade, or a century ago.

That, of course, is the supreme justification for the survival of the great house. It is not an art gallery; it is not a museum. It is a home, if on a titanic scale. The very haphazardness of the collections, the changes of fashion that dictate the enlargement of this room, the elimination of that, the introduction of this piece of domestic equipment or the elimination of that, are a precious record of the passage of time. And at the heart of the house is 'the family'. It is precisely this subtle link between the house and the same genetic group that has inhabited it for perhaps centuries, which saves the English country house from becoming a mausoleum, like so many of the châteaux of France. The Gowers Report, commissioned by the government in 1948 to study the problem of such houses, came to the conclusion that they were kept alive by the presence of their families, 'That the owner of the house is almost always the best person to preserve it. . . .'

But how to ensure the continuance of such a symbiosis? The Treasury of the British government was brought round to the realization that the country houses of the kingdom formed part of the national heritage – part indeed of its stock in trade in an era of increasing tourism – and that somebody, somewhere, has to pay for them. As early as 1910 the Inland Revenue was able to accept property in lieu of taxes; but it was not until 1946, under a Socialist government, that a Land Fund was set up which compensated the Treasury for lost taxes, and so allowed the nation itself to acquire control of houses while allowing the families to continue to live in them. In return, public access on a reasonable basis had to be allowed.

The National Trust was employed as the major piece of machinery to bring about the transfer. But the Trust provides only one way out of the dilemma, and in the eyes of many it is by no means an ideal solution. Superbly maintained though their houses might be, inevitably they become institutionalized.

Perhaps more effective in the long run is the action of the Historic Buildings Councils, set up by the Gowers Report. The Councils are empowered to make grants for essential repairs, in return for a minimum number of days of public access each year.

Increasingly, tourism is vital to the survival of these houses whether directly in terms of admission fees, or indirectly as a condition of government aid. There is, however, an increasingly healthy tendency for houses to draw on their own resources: Blenheim, Beaulieu and Knole have all established educational officers who, working with the local authority, are exploiting these houses' most priceless asset – their status as living history.

And over the past decade or so a hopeful new phenomenon has become apparent – the return to such houses of younger people, heirs of those who had abandoned or rented them a generation or more ago. The return is, perhaps, partly motivated by the rise in agricultural revenues which makes maintenance economically more possible. But it seems to be motivated too by that growing interest, amounting almost to an obsession, which our society has in preserving the past. These new owners face a formidable task. In most cases they have given up well paid careers; now new skills are demanded of them – that of accountant, hotelier, historian, caterer, and frequently farmer. The returns are mostly limited to the right to maintain genetic continuity, to live in the house where one's ancestors were born. In the best British manner we have established a compromise which is working, but only just – a kind of holding operation. The shape of the final solution is not yet visible, much less the means of acquiring it.

The houses in this book are arranged in chronological order of style. Although the living house changes its form century by century, or even decade by decade, certain dominant characteristics do remain which allow the house to be slotted into a particular period. It is these characteristics which determine their place in the present book. Thus Callaly Castle, though externally seventeenth century, is placed in the earlier period because of its possession of a pele tower, while Arundel Castle, though founded in the eleventh century, is here placed in the nineteenth century because of its interior decoration. By this means it is hoped to provide a bird's eye view of the development of the great house in England over some nine centuries.

THE MIDDLE AGES

BAMBURGH CASTLE, NORTHUMBERLAND

16 miles (25.7 km) N of Alnwick,
6 miles (9.6 km) from Belford,
3 miles (4.8 km) from Seahouses

BAMBURGH presents one of those extraordinary contrasts in which England excels. The meandering coastal road enters a tiny village that has been somewhat prettified, with mown verges, antique shops and teashops. But rearing up from the neat lawns is a vast castle of rose-coloured stone, like some mythological monster trapped in time. From its battlements you can see Lindisfarne, the Holy Island on which owners of the castle established a monastery that became a centre of learning while

The Cross Hall at Bamburgh Castle, with its rich panelling and fine Flemish tapestries.

England sank into darkness and chaos. Close to the castle gate is the Grace Darling museum, touchingly amateur, but for that very reason conveying with stark drama the story of elemental strife between land and sea that characterizes this wild coast.

The great rock to which the castle clings has been inhabited throughout history. The Romans, with a lively eye for a good military site, certainly used it: recent archaeological evidence shows that a beacon was established here. It enters recorded history in AD 547 when it became the seat of Ida, an Anglo-Saxon king, and it remained a royal stronghold for the next 1,000 years. The kings of Northumbria made it their seat until it was sacked by the Vikings. William the Conqueror lost no time in raising an enormous fortification on this rock that dominated the coastal route between England and Scotland – most of the existing external work is Norman. Many kings of England stayed here and John Baliol, the last king of Scotland, made his submission here.

During the Wars of the Roses Bamburgh succumbed to the artillery of Edward IV, the first castle in England to do so. The thunder of those guns marked the end of all castles as defensive sites. But the Crown still held on to Bamburgh, though it was allowed to fall into dilapidation. In the eighteenth century it passed into private hands and became the object of a remarkable social experiment – a kind of miniature welfare state run by the Archdeacon of Northumberland as a charity. But endowments proved inadequate; in 1894 the trustees sold the castle to the armaments millionaire Lord Armstrong, and he immediately put forward an immense programme of restoration and rebuilding.

Armstrong's work represented 'the acme of expenditure with the nadir of intelligent achievement'

The silhouette of Bamburgh Castle. This great rock has been guarded throughout history.

– the caustic judgement of an architectural historian. Certainly this romantic attempt to recreate a medieval fortress would be rejected by a modern archaeologist as inaccurate, but time has mellowed earlier criticisms. For this is the Victorian idea of a medieval castle, which is interesting to compare with Alnwick – the Victorian idea of a Renaissance palace, or Arundel – the Victorian idea of 'Gothic' Christianity.

The Great, or King's Hall at Bamburgh is an excellent example of the process adopted. The finish is Victorian, but the shape of the Hall itself is that which was revealed when the eighteenth-century additions were removed. The carved ceiling is entirely in the medieval spirit for it is the artistry of one man, Thomas Worsnop, who worked for years at Cragside, Lord Armstrong's seat. Armstrong's own portrait in the Hall sums up the man and his dream. Wearing peer's robes, he is pointing at a plan of the castle, a curious medley of the medieval and the modern but as true to its day as Pugin's Houses of Parliament were to the previous generation.

BERKELEY CASTLE, GLOUCESTERSHIRE

ENGLISH history is replete with grisly political murders, but there can be few to equal that which took place in Berkeley Castle in 1327. The deposed king, Edward II, had been handed into the safe-keeping of Thomas, Lord Berkeley – an honourable man but with no special love for the fallen monarch, and therefore deemed a good gaoler until the king's future was decided. But Edward's adulterous wife, the infamous Isabella, and her lover Mortimer wanted the impasse resolved. And so it was.

The centuries have changed the room in which Edward met his death – except for one detail. In a corner there is a deep and sinister hole. Well-attested accounts have it that corpses both of men and animals were thrown into the hole, breeding a pestilence that usually proved fatal to the prisoner. But Edward survived. Marlowe, who loved a gory tale, picked up the story in his tragedy *Edward II*, in which two turnkeys speculate on the reason for the king's survival. One says to the other:

> Yesternight, I opened but the door to throw
> him meat
> And I almost stifled by the savour

Indirect methods failing, direct murder was decided upon. The account of the method varies: Marlowe has it that the wretched man was stamped to death beneath a table. John Trevisa, who was almost certainly resident in the castle at the time,

The main entrance to the castle, set in an octagonal tower in the inner courtyard.

declared that Edward was hideously murdered 'with a hoote broche [spike] put through the secret place posterialle'. The screams of the dying man, it was said, could be heard in the town – a manifest impossibility considering the thickness of the castle's walls and the distance of the town, but attesting to the horror that the story aroused. Lord Berkeley was not present at the time of the murder – a diplomatic absence, in all probability. Altogether, this was an uncharacteristically violent episode in the centuries-long history of a family whose name has usually been associated with peace, and whose members bore such soubriquets as the Wise, the Magnanimous and the Makepeace.

Certain family names have a popular significance

The wretched Edward II was imprisoned in this room, and was horribly murdered here in 1327.

quite irrelevant to their historical weight. Berkeley is such a name. Whether it is because of a London square immortalized in a sentimental song, an exclusive London hotel or, more likely, the famous hounds, the name sets up familiar echoes in an English ear. The family, in fact, is one of the few to bridge that violent discontinuity created by the Norman Conquest. Its direct founder, Robert Fitzhardinge, was a grandson of one of Edward the Confessor's horse-thanes. He was wise enough to support Henry II against Stephen (the Berkeleys usually had the ability to spot the winner) and was granted the already massive castle in 1153. He probably rebuilt the keep immediately; it still dominates the structure, though there is a breach in it now, imposed by the Parliamentarians during the Civil War. It can be repaired only by express permission of Parliament, permission that has neither been sought nor granted, so that what was once a mark of disfavour is now a mark of historic distinction.

In certain lights the immense building seems to float on the green sea of its surrounding meadows. Those innocent fields, in fact, were part of its highly efficient defences for they could swiftly be flooded at need. Gertrude Jekyll, that eminently practical, literally down-to-earth gardener, launched into near poetry when describing the castle: 'When the day is coming to its close, and the light becomes a little dim and thin mist-films arise from the meadows, it might be an enchanted castle, for in some trick of evening light it cheats the eye into something ethereal, without substance, built up for the moment into towering masses of pearly vapour.' The beautiful colour of its stone, described as being that of potpourri, rose petals mixed with lavender, is a combination of pink sandstone and blue-grey tufa, which together give that ethereal quality.

The castle is, and always has been a living home, and each generation has made the changes thought necessary for comfort and ease. But no interior decorator has been unleashed upon the place, no Earl of Berkeley has returned from travels in Italy determined to transform his Gloucestershire castle into a Roman or Venetian palazzo. The dimensions of the rooms remain much as they were built: the Great Hall in particular is a perfect example of early fourteenth-century architecture. Passages twist and wind, windows give sudden, unexpected views – the Middle Ages still remain upon the place.

Berkeley Castle – built to dominate the river Severn. The softly mottled colouring of the castle's stonework is produced by a combination of sandstone and tufa.

The Great Hall, built on the site of the original hall about 1340. The roof is contemporary,

but was repaired in 1497. The screen has 16th-century decorations.

STOKESAY CASTLE, SHROPSHIRE

8 miles (12.8 km) from Ludlow,
¾ mile (1.2 km) s of Craven Arms off A49

DESPITE its grandiose name, this is not a castle but a fortified manor house – and far more interesting for that very reason. Castles are common enough in England, but most of the earlier manor houses have been transformed out of all recognition, where they have not been demolished outright and rebuilt in the fashionable eighteenth-century idiom. Built in the late thirteenth century, abandoned in the early nineteenth century and sensitively restored in the late nineteenth century, Stokesay Castle is a survivor from a vanished world.

A family called Say had their 'stoke', or dairy farm here about 1115. The tower was built a century later, its lower two storeys being the oldest examples of stonework at the castle. Most of the building of the manor, however, was the work of Lawrence, a wool merchant, who made his fortune in nearby Ludlow, and decided about 1281 to put his money in the land. Stokesay later came into the hands of the first Lord Craven, and as a result was besieged during the Civil War, Craven being an ardent Royalist. But not ardent enough, it seems, to watch his home being destroyed for a lost cause, and it was surrendered hastily to Parliamentary forces in 1645. Following the normal practice of 'slighting', the massive curtain walls were reduced to less than a third of their original height.

Over the next century, frequent sub-leasing of the manor to local families caused it to become ever more dilapidated. By 1814, it was unequivocally described as 'abandoned to neglect and rapidly advancing to ruin'. In 1869 it was bought by John Darby Allcroft who, in a remarkably public-spirited manner, thoroughly restored it though without any intention of living in it. His descendants have also accepted responsibility for maintaining it although it remains empty, apart from the gatehouse.

The visitor receives two quite different impressions on entering the courtyard. Standing with one's back to the gatehouse and looking across what is now a green lawn, one sees an ecclesiastical-looking range of stone buildings flanked by towers. To the north is the original tower built by the Says while the other, known as the South Tower, was

Stokesay, seen across the flower-spangled churchyard, with its towers and contrasting Elizabethan gatehouse.

The solar to which the family withdrew for privacy. Begun about 1285, its contents date from the 17th century.

begun by Lawrence of Ludlow. The range in-between consists of the Great Hall and the Solar wing which form the heart of Stokesay, and was also mostly Lawrence's work. ,

But turning round, one is immediately transported forward several centuries, for the gatehouse is a comfortable half-timbered Elizabethan dwelling, and the encircling stone walls serve only as a demarcation between the courtyard and the rolling Shropshire hills. Before they were slighted they would have towered up to at least half the height of the original stone gatehouse, creating security but also a decidedly gloomy and claustrophobic courtyard.

To enter the Great Hall is to receive a sudden and dramatic correction to the popular idea of the romantic delights of medieval life. This is where the lord of the manor dined with his family and retainers, where they gathered to pass the endless hours in inclement weather. And it is simply a great barn. The roof timbers high overhead disappear into shadow even on a bright day, and the rafters in the centre are still blackened from the smoke of the hearth below. There is no sign of a chimney. It needs little imagination to reconstruct the hall as it must have appeared on a winter's night – a great cavern, swept by icy draughts, choked with smoke. The lord and his lady were only too aware of those killing draughts: their high table was set as far as possible from the door.

The contrast between hall and solar could not be more marked. The solar, here as elsewhere, was the response to the growing desire of the family to have some privacy, some other, smaller chamber where it was possible to introduce an element of comfort. The undercroft of the solar block was used as cellarage and storage. The solar proper was on the second floor, reached by an external staircase outside the hall. The naked stone walls of the room were panelled in the seventeenth century but one can still look beyond this later refinement and see what this room would have offered those taking refuge from the Great Hall. The low ceiling creates at least an impression of snugness, and the large windows are designed to let in the sunshine which gives its name to this type of chamber (*solarium*).

BROUGHTON CASTLE, OXFORDSHIRE

2 miles (3.2 km) SW of Banbury
on the Shipton-on-Stour road (B4035)

AMONG the treasures of this friendly, moated manor house (which Henry James described as 'the most delightful home in England') are two unassuming little volumes, one of them bound in vellum. They constitute the original manuscript of that indefatigable young lady, Celia Fiennes, whose spirit of sheer curiosity took her the length and breadth of seventeenth-century England, accompanied only by a man servant. Her journal, with its breathless, high-spirited prose, provides a view into a vanished England – which, she says, with splendid xenophobia, 'will cure the evil itch of over-valuing foreign parts'.

Although born in Wiltshire, Celia Fiennes was related to the Fiennes family who owned Broughton Castle (and who, three centuries later, still do). She naturally stayed in the houses of her relatives and friends whenever possible, and her testimony provides priceless first-hand evidence of the social life of her day. What she has to say of Broughton Castle, her grandfather's seat, is not very flattering, expressed in her typically, unpunctuated style. 'It's an old house moted all round and a park and gardens but are much left to decay and ruin, when my brother came to it.'

The house (for house it is, despite its martial title) was a good 300 years old when she visited it, for it was begun in the late fourteenth century by a Sir John de Broughton. Although its moat is not as picturesque as those at Ightham and Hever, it is decidedly more impressive – a great sheet of water almost wide enough to be called a lake. The only

A typical fortified manor house. The gatehouse controlled the only access – the bridge across the moat.

The Star Chamber, with its hand-painted Chinese wallpaper.

access to the house is across a bridge and through a massive gatehouse. Most of the curtain wall that was built along the line of the moat in the early fifteenth century has been demolished, but one is most vividly aware of being at the heart of a defended complex that was well able to look after its own. The Fiennes acquired the house by marriage in 1451 and about a century later transformed it from a manor house, built for protection, into a family mansion. This is the appearance that it gives today, but the original medieval building is everywhere evident – most noticeably in the Great Hall.

In a modest little room on the upper floor of one of the towers, the course of English history was changed. There, between 1629 and 1640, William, Lord Saye, and others opposed to Charles I met to plan their campaign (under the pretext of being members of the Providence Island Company). Nicknamed Old Subtlety, William has had a bad press. Contemporary historians (mostly Cavalier) loathed him: for the great Clarendon he was 'proud, morose and of a sullen nature, one who had conversed much with books ... who lived sordidly in the country'. But though a Puritan, Lord Saye was no Leveller: it is more than likely that, like many a would-be reformer before him, he was overtaken by events – the man who started an avalanche by removing a pebble.

Broughton Castle has changed little over the years. It was saved from the worst excesses of nineteenth-century 'restoration' by the profligate young fifteenth Baron. In 1837 the castle was virtually stripped of its contents – even the swans on the moat were sold. The auctioneer's catalogue, with the prices realized, shows that objects were sold for pence rather than pounds. The art collec-

tion was dispersed for ridiculous sums. There may be room to doubt the authenticity of the Bruegel sold for £2 19s, but not the Knellers or the Lelys which went for a guinea each.

Subsequently, the house passed through the hands of various tenants before returning again to the family, who determined to make it support itself. The house is, in effect, divided into two. The private rooms are a delightful mixture of the casually intimate and the historic: the ceiling of the kitchen, is of bare thirteenth-century stone sheltering highly efficient twentieth-century equipment; and a newly-built circular staircase, traditional in shape but modern in substance, connects upper and lower floors. But there is no sense of a museum in either private or public section: children of the present Lord and Lady Saye were brought up in the Chinese Room with its rare and vulnerable wallpaper. The beautiful Long Gallery was recently restored by John Fowler, creating new wallpaper out of antique blocks, using a warm orange colour that echoes the Oxfordshire ploughland visible through the windows. And summing up the symbiosis of new and old is the immense new carpet in the Oak Room, paid for by a film company who used the castle as their setting.

The spectacular ceiling of the Great Parlour, dated 1599.

PENSHURST PLACE, KENT

In Penshurst village, 7 miles (11.2 km)
S of Sevenoaks-Tunbridge Wells road,
3½ miles (5.6 km) W of Tonbridge on B2176

'I AM the greengrocer. I live over my shop', the owner of Penshurst Place remarked, during a discussion about the problems of maintaining and living in a great country house in the last quarter of the twentieth century. One is tempted to paraphrase the wartime Churchillian phrase 'Some greengrocer! Some shop!' For the shopkeeper is Lord De L'Isle VC, KG, and the shop is his immense extended home – half country house, half castle – which centres on a medieval manor house still intact after more than six centuries.

Penshurst, the birth place of Sir Philip Sidney and still in the possession of the Sidney family, demonstrates that there is no one answer to the problem of conservation and survival. Lord De L'Isle refuses to accept government grants for repairs, arguing that this leads to loss of independence. And where other houses are tied closely to their estates, at Penshurst estate and house have been separated. Lord De L'Isle believes that house and garden must be run as a business, generating if possible its own income. 'An agricultural estate is, at best, no more than self-balancing economically and can easily be drained financially if it is too closely bound to a great house in a single management unit.'

There has been a garden at Penshurst for at least six centuries, its outward form undergoing many changes. But neither Capability Brown nor Humphrey Repton arrived here to put their bland, homogenizing touch on everything. The great protecting walls, begun in 1570, have survived. But the gardens, restored during the nineteenth century, deteriorated again during World War II and have been under course of restoration ever since. Now they form a great series of carefully planted hedges and walled enclosures – a renaissance of the formal English garden. Other attractions are an imaginative adventure playground for the young and a permanent exhibition of agricultural implements and machinery.

The house itself is a classic example of organic growth. The great Baron's Hall was built between

The Baron's Hall with its screen and minstrels' gallery.

The helmet of Sir Philip Sidney.

The south front showing the original curtain wall, defensive Garden Tower (right) and central Great Hall.

1338 and 1349. Half a century later it was enclosed in a curtain wall that gives an outline as clear and exact as that of a child's fort. Over the next two centuries, more buildings budded off from the Baron's Hall, creeping towards the encircling wall. No longer required as defence it slowly disappeared in most places, though some of the towers were incorporated within the residential building.

But throughout all this, the Baron's Hall remained unchanged. It is different in degree, though not in kind, from Stokesay so that one can see here the last flowering of that great, primitive meeting place, the hall, which is at the heart of all medieval dwellings. The screen that masks the serving doors is still a simple wooden screen, though on an immense scale; the lord's dais still remains; the great hearth is still central. A fire of logs occasionally warms twentieth-century visitors as it warmed kings, princes and feudal lords as they dined at high table in the Middle Ages. And from the huge, naked but curiously friendly chamber great stone steps wind up to another civilization, for they lead to the dining room that appears, by contrast, to belong to our own time.

This gallery at Penshurst was added in the 1820s.

RABY CASTLE, DURHAM

1 mile (1.6 km) N of Staindrop village
on Barnard Castle-Bishop Auckland road (A688)

EVEN today, when time has mellowed the stone and set the whole in gentle parkland, the first and last impression of Raby is of an enormous, almost brutal strength. This is still a castle, despite the fact that centuries have passed since it last saw military action. The towers rear up, spiky with turrets, toothed with crenellations. There are nine of them altogether, each with its own identity and distinctive history, linked together by the curtain wall. Passing through the gateway, the visitor is immediately confronted by the massive Clifford's Tower; the biggest tower of all it was specifically designed to protect the gateway, or render it untenable if it was taken. Beyond is the oddly-shaped Bulmer's Tower; where all its neighbours are rectangular, this is leaf-shaped, or perhaps more appropriately, like a spear facing southward. Time has cast its

The richly decorated octagonal drawing room at Raby.

homogenizing mantle over it, but Bulmer's Tower is probably the oldest part of this ancient castle. Tradition claims that its bottom course is the work of no less a person than Canute – 'Emperor of the North' as he called himself – and certainly he had his seat at Raby.

The octagonal Kitchen Tower, curiously domestic in this range of military might, has not changed since it was first built in the fourteenth century. While state rooms and the family's lodgings may alter from century to century in accordance with the whim of fashion, domestic quarters change only slowly in great houses. Why change a kitchen or a brewery except to make it bigger or for better access?

Tracing a legendary descent from Canute's niece, the Nevills ruled here for nearly 400 years, until the fatal Great Rising of the North in 1569. On that occasion the Catholic barons decided to rebel in favour of Mary, Queen of Scots. Their plot – which was to cost most of them dear, above all, the last Nevill – was hatched in this very same castle. Wordsworth romanticized the occasion:

> Seven hundred knights, retainers all
> Of Nevill, at their master's call
> Had sate together in Raby's Hall

Part of the original medieval building, the Hall owes its present appearance to Carr's work of 1781.

The Hall has changed considerably in appearance.

Raby's many-towered skyline, each tower with a clear identity. The immense curtain wall is thirty feet high.

William Burn (1789–1870), the Victorian architect, gave it the fashionable neo-Gothic look together with a splendid new ceiling, and lengthened it by some seventy feet. But looking down this immense stretch is to realize that Wordsworth scarcely exaggerated. It was indeed quite likely that 700 men gathered here. They were by no means unanimous about the proposed rebellion against Queen Elizabeth, but the Lady of Raby goaded them on – and lost her estate for her pains. The Crown cannily held the castle for over fifty years until Sir Henry Vane bought it in 1626, and his descendants hold it today as the Lords Barnard.

The interior was much altered by John Carr of York in the 1780s. His work is to be found all over the north, but there is nothing to equal the extent of his alterations here, the most bizarre being the adaptation of the entrance hall. The inner court of Raby is surprisingly small, too small for a horse and carriage to turn around, so Carr altered the hall enabling a horse and carriage to pass *through* it. Most of the castle's furnishing is post-eighteenth century, the result of one of the blazing family rows that characterize so many great houses. The first Lord Barnard was so furious when his son married without his permission that, in 1741, he sold off everything moveable, chopped down all the trees in the park – and even contemplated demolishing the building. But the characteristic white-painted cottages of the estate remain; once they are out of sight, the visitor knows that he has left the lands of the Lord Barnard.

HADDON HALL, DERBYSHIRE

2 miles (3.2 km) S of Bakewell,
6½ miles (10.4 km) N of Matlock on A6

PARADOXICALLY, neglect preserved Haddon Hall unchanged for posterity. In the early eighteenth century its owners, the dukes of Rutland, abandoned it for their grander house – Belvoir Castle. Haddon, lost among its Derbyshire hills, dreamed on while the outside world went on its racketing way. When Celia Fiennes visited the house in 1697 she emphasized the remoteness of the countryside; certainly, only a tough and curious-minded traveller like herself would deliberately seek out such a place. 'You are forced to have guides: the common people know not above two or three miles from their home.' She thought Haddon not particularly remarkable – 'a good old house all built of stone but nothing very curious as the mode now is'.

That final phrase of hers – 'nothing very curious as the mode now is' – is the key to the interest that Haddon holds for us today. While other houses were going through the drastic rebuilding of the eighteenth century, or the no less drastic restorations of the nineteenth century, Haddon was left untouched except for maintenance. It was not until 1924 that the Marquis of Granby (later the ninth Duke of Rutland) moved to Haddon and made its restoration his life's work. Part of the building is used today as a hunting lodge or holiday home. But most of it is empty, giving the visitor an unrivalled opportunity to inspect a house which developed between the late eleventh and the early seventeenth centuries.

The history of Haddon Hall goes back to the beginning of English history, for William the Conqueror gave the original manor to an illegitimate son, William Peverel. His descendants lost the estate during the civil wars of the twelfth century,

Sir Henry Vernon built this room as his 'parlour' in 1500. The painted ceiling is contemporary, although carefully restored in 1926.

The chapel, with its Norman arches and font, contains several fifteenth-century murals including this fine portrayal of St Christopher striding through the river, and two of St Nicholas.

and it came into the hands of the Vernons who were to hold it for 400 years. According to legend, a daughter of the Vernons, Lady Dorothy, eloped with her lover, John Manners, during the wedding festivities of her sister in the Long Gallery. Whatever the truth of the story, Lady Dorothy Vernon did indeed marry John Manners, later Duke of Rutland. Thus, one of the great romances of the sixteenth century was instrumental in transmitting the estate to its present owners.

The house, in its idyllic setting, is reached over a seventeenth-century bridge across the rushing river Wye and then up a steep and winding lane, the very epitome of the approach to a medieval castle. Restoration has been done with extreme care and subtlety. What appears to be a perfectly carved runnel in the entrance porch, for example, is stone worn by centuries of footsteps. Beyond the gatehouse is the kind of physical evidence of the changing past that makes Haddon so fascinating, even to the layman. Where the south wall joins the gatehouse, it looks as though amateur masons, working without direction, have produced a hodge-podge of styles. The apparent confusion, however, is the result of trying to abut a new wall, running down a slope, to an existing wall. In most other houses, this kind of evidence has been smoothed away.

Haddon is thus a three-dimensional textbook of medieval architecture. In the tall, narrow chapel, the observant eye can find evidence of almost every century since it was begun by the Normans. Here, again, the paradox of neglect as a preservative is demonstrated. The Puritans, in their anxiety to shield the eyes of the faithful from ungodly images, whitewashed the exquisite medieval murals. They were thus protected until the whitewash was removed during twentieth-century restorations.

Haddon Hall is built on a hill, the 17th-century gardens descending by splendid stone terraces to the river.

All through the house is this sense of the past impinging on the present, most immediately and most poignantly perhaps in the kitchens. Carbon deposits from the rushlights can still be detected – by touch as well as sight – on the walls. The great bake ovens are of a kind that were still in use in Derbyshire well within living memory. Wood shapes the place: on one wall a vast baulk has been carved into two basins; in the centre of the floor is the starkly-named killing block – a massive piece of

The oak-panelled Long Gallery.

wood with a crude hole bored through it. A rope, passed through this, forced the animal's head down onto the block where it could be dispatched, as witnessed by the many deep grooves in the wood.

The Banqueting Hall retains the dais which allowed the lord and his family to be psychologically separate from, though sharing the same room with, their retainers. The splendid roof timbers are new, part of the 1924 restoration. Hidden in one of them is a leaden box giving precise details of the restorations for the benefit of posterity.

But it is in the Long Gallery that time has really been frozen. Dorothy Vernon would have known this room, for it was built by her father and has remained quite unchanged. Even on a dull day it is flooded with light: the curious distortions of the diamond window panes throughout the house are deliberate, an ingenious device to catch light at all angles. Over the centuries, idlers have scratched their initials and varying sentiments on the glass. Here, above all, the beauty of wood emerges in its own right, faded now to a beautiful silver-grey, and unobscured by pictures except the curiously moving landscape painted by Rex Whistler in 1933, showing the ninth Duke and his son looking down on this beautiful, lonely house.

BEAULIEU PALACE HOUSE, HAMPSHIRE

In Beaulieu 5 miles (8 km) SE of Lyndhurst

ST BERNARD of Clairvaux, the founder of the first Cistercian abbey in Burgundy in 1098, deliberately chose a remote and isolated site. He advised his followers to do likewise. 'Trust one who has tried it', he wrote. 'You will find more in words than in books.' The great abbey of Beaulieu, founded in 1204 under the patronage of King John, was established in an isolated corner of the New Forest, already known as Beau Lieu, or 'beautiful place'.

When the monastery was dissolved in 1538, it was bought by Thomas Wriothesley, later the first Earl of Southampton, for £1,350 6s 8d. Most of the buildings were demolished, and the stone was used to build castles to guard the Solent. But the monks' refectory became the parish church, whilst the Great Gatehouse was adapted as a manor house. It was altered again in the 1720s, and considerably enlarged in the 1870s by the architect Sir Reginald Blomfield for Lord Henry Scott, later first Baron Montagu of Beaulieu. Palace House today has the outward appearance of 'Scots baronial', but the interior is a remarkable mixture of the fourteenth and nineteenth centuries. In the Upper Drawing Room, for example, both a piscina and an aumbry still exist, while in the Dining Room there is a fourteenth-century bread cupboard, probably the oldest piece of furniture in the house. Thus the possessions of medieval abbots mingle with those of nineteenth-century lords of the manor.

Beaulieu is one of the great houses which has adopted tourism as a means of financial viability. The attractions of medieval abbey and of manor house were augmented in 1952 when Lord Montagu opened his collection of vintage cars to the public. This developed into the National Motor Museum, now owned by a trust.

Beaulieu Palace House, with the original Great Gatehouse of the abbey at the heart of a complex which took on its Victorian Gothic shape between 1870 and 1873.

An altar once stood in this Upper Drawing Room, immediately below the far east window. On the right is the piscina in which the priest washed the chalice.

Now the main Dining Room, this was originally the Inner Hall of the gatehouse. The 14th-century bread cupboard still survives.

At Beaulieu, museum, tourist and residential roles are all interlocked. An outstanding project has been the gradual excavation and restoration of the abbey ruins under professional direction, together with research into the life of the now vanished monastic community. Although Beaulieu may be part of the world of entertainment, it also has more serious functions. An education service was established in 1972, and countless school children are given an insight into living history. The house has been arranged as one large diorama, with the visitors somehow a part of it. In most of the rooms there are historic figures, from 1538 onwards, wearing appropriate costume, illustrating either some aspect of the house's history or furnishing in a series of tableaux.

If Longleat pioneered the idea of opening to the public, and Woburn took that to its logical conclusion, Beaulieu was probably the first to capitalize on the fact that education can be a profoundly absorbing activity, to be enjoyed rather than endured.

The ecclesiastical origins of Palace House.

ST MICHAEL'S MOUNT, CORNWALL

½ mile (0.80 km) from the shore at Marazion (A394),
connected by causeway; 3 miles (4.8 km) E Penzance
The National Trust

THE castle-capped island rears up from the waters of Mount's Bay like a vision from an Arthurian romance – but this island was colonized at least a millenium before Arthur was born. It is almost certainly the island of Ictis, where continental traders picked up the Cornish tin bound for the Mediterranean. Writing about AD 20 Diodorus, the Greek historian, picked on the phenomenon which made the island particularly useful. 'During the ebb tide the intervening space [between island and coast] is left dry and they carry over to the island the tin in abundance in their wagons.'

At ebb tide now there is a handsome rough causeway, laid down about 1425 by the monks who erected the first permanent buildings on the island.

By carefully judging the time of arrival, the traveller can stroll across – and it is a decidedly curious experience to enter a port on foot from the seaward side. A path winds steeply upward, through banks of flowers, towards the massive steps, carved from the rock itself, by which the castle is entered. By the side of the path, roughly halfway up, is a deep well which figures in that enduring folk story – Jack the Giant Killer. The Mount was supposedly built by a giant called Cormoran, a great stealer of mainland cattle, until Jack dug a pit and enticed him into it.

The atmosphere of legend, of fairy tale, lingers throughout St Michael's Mount. Building has been in progress on the crest for over seven centuries, from 1135 when the first priory was built, to the

The Blue Drawing Room, converted c. 1740 from the 15th-century Lady Chapel and decorated in Gothic style.

The early morning sun outlines the building – part castle, part church, part home – an integral element of the Mount.

Victorian addition of 1878. But because the builders all used the same material – granite – and because they adopted similar solutions when faced with the same constructional problem – how to fit a building on to a crag – the whole seems one great structure.

St Michael's Mount was a daughter of that other island priory across the Channel, Mont St Michel. The problem of the dual loyalty of its monks was solved when, in 1424, control was handed over to Syon Abbey. At the dissolution, the Crown retained control of so important a military site, leasing it to carefully vetted governors. In 1647 a Parliamentary colonel, John St Aubyn, was nominated Governor and bought the island in 1659. Descendants of St Aubyn, enobled as Lords St Levan, continued to hold both the buildings and the island until 1954, when they gave St Michael's Mount to the National Trust with a substantial endowment, although the Lords St Levan still reside there.

This is no make-believe castle, despite its picturesque appearance. Its long history has been punctuated by sieges, rebellions and occupations. Perkin Warbeck, the Pretender to the throne, found refuge here with his beautiful 'queen', Catherine, in 1497. Sir Francis Bassett, the King's Governor, honourably defended it against Parliamentary forces in 1642. It was militarily active as late as 1812 when its guns dismasted a French frigate, and even in World War II it had a strong garrison, and was machine-gunned from the air.

The main entrance to the castle. Having made the steep ascent to the left, one enters by the low, solid door in the centre, with the rock falling away sheer behind.

The Chevy Chase Room. Originally the refectory of the monastery, the roof timbers are 15th century. The frieze of hunting scenes gives this room its name.

The great, rambling building began to be properly adapted to residential purposes in the mid-nineteenth century. An entire new wing was built in the 1870s, but in general the existing ancient building was preserved and modern comforts and interior decorations were imprinted upon it. The Chevy Chase Room which takes it name from the frieze of hunting scenes, is the original twelfth-century refectory whose fifteenth-century roof was restored in the nineteenth century. Most remarkable, perhaps is the conversion of the fifteenth-century Lady Chapel into a drawing room in the mid-eighteenth century. The views from it are superb, for it looks out immediately upon the north terrace on the very summit of the island. But, despite its elegance, it must, one feels, have been a cold and comfortless place.

IGHTHAM MOTE, KENT

2½ miles (4 km) s of Ightham off A227,
6 miles (9.6 km) E of Sevenoaks

THE meaning of the first part of this curious name is straightforward enough, for it is the name of the nearby village of Ightham. In the infuriating English manner, however, the house is actually in the village of Ivy Hatch. But does 'mote' mean a meeting place, as has been suggested? Or is it a more likely reference to the moat which surrounds this exquisite manor house? It is all of a piece with the uncertainty that hangs over much of its history.

Some houses change hands only rarely: at Ightham Mote there have been seven families in six centuries, three of them in the seventy years between 1521 and 1591. Its survival today is due to a remarkable act of disinterested generosity on the part of an American. The last owner of the house had died in 1950, and when it came on the market a group of local businessmen bought it to prevent it falling into the wrong hands. In 1953 Charles Henry Robinson, a businessman from Portland, Maine, made a bid for it. It is said that returning home by sea he changed his mind, and wrote a letter cancelling the bid – but forgot to post it. Although domiciled in America, he directed the restoration of the house over the following years and subsequently made arrangements for it to be left to the National Trust on his death.

Visiting ancient houses one after another, one is tempted to escalate superlatives, but Ightham Mote really is a jewel. It is difficult to find, although less than twenty-five miles from London, for it is tucked away in a private little valley down narrow Kentish lanes. Apart from the fourteenth-century gatehouse

The courtyard is a fascinating melange of periods and styles, from the 14th-century stone hall on the right to the 19th-century dog's kennel close by. The oriel window is 16th century, inserted in what was the solar.

The main entrance with its 15th-century doors.

The 14th-century Hall arches rest on carved corbels.

it does not pretend to be a castle, as do other moated manor houses, but is simply a large private house, surrounded by a walled moat that is the delight of neighbouring ducks. The first builder was Sir Thomas Cawne, whose armour-clad effigy is in the parish church. Over some thirty years, before his death in 1374, he had built perhaps half the existing house, including the lower part of the gatehouse, the moat and the Great Hall. The latter was to undergo considerable changes, the last in 1872 when Norman Shaw was commissioned to make it habitable according to nineteenth-century standards. This was the period when a seated female skeleton was found walled up in a cupboard, her age, identity and the motive for the bizarre occurrence all being unknown.

Subsequent owners continued the building, gradually creating a delightful square courtyard dominated by the Tudor additions of Richard Clement in 1521. It was during this time that the house gained a most unusual, and today probably unique feature – the barrel vault of the chapel. The vault is made up of alternating wooden panels carrying various badges and motifs – the rose of York, the arrows of Aragon, the portcullis of Beaufort (now the arms of Westminster City Council) and others. They are now much faded, although an imaginative recreation of one section gives an idea of the colourful, not to say gaudy, impression of the original. Such ceilings were made for the elaborate temporary pavilions used during ceremonial outdoor events of which there were many, such as the Field of the Cloth of Gold, and this may well be a survivor.

*One of the stone figure corbels
in the Hall.*

The walled moat extends round the entire house, fed by a clear stream.

THE FIFTEENTH CENTURY

GREAT DIXTER, EAST SUSSEX

½ mile (0.80 km) N of Northiam, 8 miles (12.8 km) NW of Rye,
12 miles (19.3 km) N of Hastings, just off A28

IN a less dramatic fashion, this is as remarkable an exercise in historical restoration as was Hever Castle. The house was all but derelict when the architectural historian, Nathaniel Lloyd, bought it in 1910. Edwin Lutyens was given the job of restoring and enlarging it, and embarked on the task shortly before he undertook his massive commission of Castle Drogo.

Great Dixter is a delightful example of a timber-framed house, that solid yeoman's home built from the oak of the great Weald that once lapped all this region of south-east England. The first recorded reference to the manor is as early as 1220, but the oldest part of the present house, the Great Hall, dates from about 1450. Lutyens restored the hall to its original dignified proportions by boldly removing floors and partitions which had been inserted after the hall was built, but were of impressive antiquity when he came to tackle the task. He enlarged the house in two entirely different ways.

Lutyens' tile-hung addition on the left is in honest contrast to the timbered front of the original building, but both parts combine to make a satisfying whole.

The front was extended in a manner which, while within the vernacular tradition of the whole building, was honestly distinct from it. Lutyens achieved this by hanging it with tiles contrasting with the half-timbering of the original building. He extended the back in a manner that was startlingly innovatory then. He found an early sixteenth-century timbered cottage at Benenden, also in a derelict state, and transported it bodily to Great Dixter, incorporating it at the rear of the house. The technique is much used today to preserve small historic buildings – particularly those in the way of road development. The entire Weald and Downland Museum at Singleton, near Chichester, is made up of such salvaged buildings, but it needed an architect of Lutyens' confidence and sensitivity to achieve this success in 1910.

He also designed the gardens, retaining many of the original farm buildings. The oast house, for instance, was in use until 1939. Seventy years after completion a family link is still maintained, for the estate is run by Quentin Lloyd, and the now famous gardens by Christopher Lloyd, sons of the man who originally saved the house.

The Wealden house displayed : the Hall at Great Dixter.

The topiary garden is also Lutyens' work, the oast houses and farm buildings of the original complex being incorporated into the design.

NORTON CONYERS, NORTH YORKSHIRE

3½ miles (5.6 km) N of Ripon near Wath,
1½ miles (2.1 km) from A1

CHARLOTTE Brontë visited Norton Conyers whilst acting as governess to some unruly children near Harrogate in 1839. Upstairs in the attics was a room to which legend clung; sometime in the previous century, a mad woman was supposed to have been confined there. This strange story stayed in Charlotte's mind and later, through the alchemy of the artist, emerged in *Jane Eyre*, with the mad woman as Mrs Rochester, and Norton Conyers as Thornfield Hall.

Norton Conyers was originally a fortified manor house. It has been continuously occupied throughout its 500-year existence and has seen many changes. The unusual roughcast which covers the exterior is misleading; it was added in the eighteenth century to protect the late fifteenth-century brickwork. But here and there the exterior shows indications of its earlier appearance: an arrowslit and battlements remind one that even in the fifteenth century a Yorkshire farmer was well advised to provide means for his protection.

The house is named after two families who successively owned it. The Conyers were Norman, acquiring large areas of land in Yorkshire and Durham as their share of the loot after the Conquest. The Nortons acquired this part of their properties by marriage in the late fourteenth century, but being ill-advised enough to take the wrong

Roughcast conceals the early brickwork which dates from the 15th century, while the distinctive curved gables date from the 17th century.

The Hall. The 19th-century painting of the Quorn Hunt shows Bellingham Graham as master.

side in the Catholic rebellion of 1569, forfeited it to the Crown. The Grahams, a Scottish family, bought the house and lands in 1624 and their descendants remain there today.

The boundary walls of grey stone still survive, providing a lively picture of the cheapness of labour before the twentieth century. All great estates had these walls, whose total length must surpass the Great Wall of China. A narrow drive leads directly to the front of the house, which is separated from the surrounding parkland by a ha-ha, that ingenious device to divide the domestic area of a house from its grounds, yet allow the one to blend visually with the other. The park is landscaped, but without flamboyance, for Norton Conyers' role in history was not that of a castle, nor of a 'prodigy house' designed to impress the monarchy, but of a manor, the heart of an agricultural estate.

The same decent reticence pervades the house. This is a home, not a showplace. The front door leads directly into the hall, whose contents are the accretion of centuries. In the centre stands the

The gateway to Norton Conyers' garden of unusual plants.

house's greatest treasure, an exceedingly rare sixteenth-century inlaid table. At one end, under an enormous picture of the Quorn Hunt, painted by John Ferneley in 1822, is a long and ancient refectory table, its surface scored with grooves cut for the purpose of playing shove ha'penny. This was last used for its designed purpose seven years ago at a family wedding; the bride's dress is on display upstairs.

A superb wooden staircase sweeps up out of the hall. On one landing there is a curious horseshoe-shaped mark. According to legend, it was made by the horse which brought one of the Grahams home from the battle of Marston Moor in 1644, where he was wounded; it galloped so hard that its shoe was red-hot on arrival. It seems an improbable story; yet the piece of wood bearing the mark has been carefully moved to its present position in order to preserve it.

Certainly the legend of the mad woman is rooted in fact. But her name, her social standing – was she a servant, or a member of the family? – are now all forgotten.

The orangery, built about 1776.

CALLALY CASTLE, NORTHUMBERLAND

2 miles (3.2 km) w of Whittingham,
10 miles (16 km) w of Alnwick

THIS solid, grey house set among the Northumbrian hills perfectly demonstrates the near impossibility of giving an exact date to any country house. A casual glance classifies it as a late seventeenth-century classical mansion and this, so far as the externals are concerned, would be accurate enough.

But within the grounds of Callaly Castle are three ancient British tombs, British earthworks, part of a Roman road and the foundations of a Norman castle. A substantial part of the house itself is a pele tower, one of the fortifications unique to this once troubled border area. Originally, a pele was simply a palisade or stockade into which cattle were driven to protect them from raiders. In the course of time the palisade evolved into a solid stone tower with cattle housed on the ground floor and humans above. And when, in time, the rule of law made such massive fortifications quite unnecessary, the tower usually served as the starting point for a purely residential building.

This was what happened at Callaly. On the left of the south front is a massive, square wing – the original pele tower built in 1415. The Saxon owners of the manor continued to live here even after the

The south front. On the extreme left is the pele tower, built about 1415, the starting point of the whole complex.

45

Norman Conquest, paying thirty shillings a year in tribute, and delivering a fully grown oak to Callaly Castle every other day from Whitsun to August for the king's hearth. A Norman family called Clavering bought the manor in 1217 and were destined to live there for 600 years. They had a turbulent history: remaining Catholic like so many of their fellow northerners, they suffered considerable penalties as a result. They also took the side of the ill-fated King Charles during the Civil War and later were involved in the 1715 rebellion, for which they were penalized yet again. Nevertheless, they seem to have been a remarkably resilient family; it was not until 1876 that, with the failure of the male line, the castle was sold to Major Alexander Browne, whose descendants hold it today. In a thousand years of history, therefore, Callaly has changed hands only three times.

The apparent regularity imposed on the building's externals in the seventeenth century is belied by the maze of passages and rooms within, for building has continued from the fifteenth to the nineteenth century. An example of the complexity awaiting the visitor who wants to unravel Callaly's architectural history is vividly shown in the guidebook's attempt to explain the development of the north front. 'This is very difficult to follow,' the guidebook says with truth. 'The original outside North Wall is now the South Wall of the passage which runs inside the castle itself, parallel to the

Detail of the Drawing Room.

North Front. The west end of the inside wall was the outside wall of the great hall, built in 1619.' The entrance to the smoking room illustrates the ad hoc manner in which the house has grown. The entrance runs through what is virtually a tunnel seven feet long and is, in fact, the immensely thick wall of the pele tower, the smoking room occupying what would have been the cattle pens five centuries ago.

In 1757, part of the south wing was gutted to make way for the rococo Drawing Room, one of the best mid-eighteenth century rooms in this style in the north. The last major additions to the castle were made in the 1890s when the Brownes acquired it. The present music room is a remarkable adaptation of a once-open courtyard that is now a prime example of Victoriana. Prominently displayed in it is the exquisite marble head of a horse. Found at Ephesus on the site of the Temple of Diana, it was part of a superb collection of marbles and objets d'árt for which an entire museum wing was built in 1891. The British Museum bought most of the collection, but this sculpture – which St Paul might well have seen – remained to create one of those curious historical links that characterize the country house.

Marble horse's head, found at Ephesus in 1841. The rest of the collection was sold to the British Museum in 1899.

The Drawing Room is on the site of the original Great Hall immediately east of the pele tower. Its present form and decoration date from 1757.

PURSE CAUNDLE MANOR, DORSET

In Purse Caundle village,
4 miles (6.4 km) E of Sherborne

THERE are few semantic delights to equal the place names of the West Country. The meaning of many even now is conjectural. As late as 1963, when Arthur Oswald was researching Purse Caundle Manor for *Country Life*, he could remark 'No one knows the meaning of its delightfully improbable name, which might have come out of some old book of country receipts. If ever there was an inhabitant called Purse, he is unknown to history.' But in August 1978, a lady visiting the manor announced 'I am born a Purse.' So she was. Painstaking research slowly disclosed that, in 1065, somebody called Purse the Elder built cottages for 175 serfs in the village of Caundle, which became known thereafter as Purse Caundle.

The manor house itself, tucked into the heart of the village, was built at least 400 years later. In the late thirteenth century a certain John Alleyn lived in a house on the site with a duty 'to keep and lodge the king's sick or injured hounds at the king's cost', but the building of the present house did not commence for another two centuries. It is a stone building, grey and mellowed, blending in with its surroundings. From the village lane to the east, it seems little more than a cottage, though with an uncommonly handsome oriel window. But this is deceptive. Successive owners, working up to the seventeenth century, greatly extended the old house, producing some odd anomalies. Why is the ceremonial Great Chamber on the service side of the house? Where was the original kitchen? A rather dull, seemingly Victorian passageway proved on examination to be the original screens passage, for the old doorways that once connected buttery and pantry with the Great Hall had been covered with plasterwork. A considerable amount of restoration was undertaken in the early twentieth century by Lady Victoria Herbert, but architecturally, Purse Caundle Manor still poses as great a puzzle as the semantics of its place name.

The size and complexity of the house, seen from the south front; it was extended westward in the 17th century.

The screens passage, with the kitchen to the right.

The oriel window on the east end of the manor.

The 15th-century Hall with its later tiebeams.

THE SIXTEENTH CENTURY

LONGLEAT HOUSE, WILTSHIRE

4 miles (6.4 km) SW of Warminster,
4½ miles (7.2 km) SE of Frome
on A362 (between Bath and Salisbury)

HENRY Thynne, sixth Marquess of Bath, was the first owner of a great house to attempt to make it pay for itself. On the death of his father in 1946, he was faced with a bill of £700,000 in death duties. Money raised by selling land staved off that immediate threat. But by the end of the 1940s it was becoming increasingly apparent that very few country houses could maintain themselves in the traditional manner. In 1947, the Marquess decided to open Longleat to the public on a fee-paying basis. It was a decided gamble. The car-owning population was still small, petrol was rationed, and it was by no means certain that so unprecedented an idea would catch on in a country still suffering from austerity. But his family supported him. Household treasures were disinterred from lofts and stables and put on display; odds and ends of liveries were put together; the great State Coach repainted, and a ground floor bedroom turned into a souvenir shop. The house was opened to the public in April 1949 at an entrance fee of 2s 6d (12½p); by the end of the year, 135,000 people had visited it.

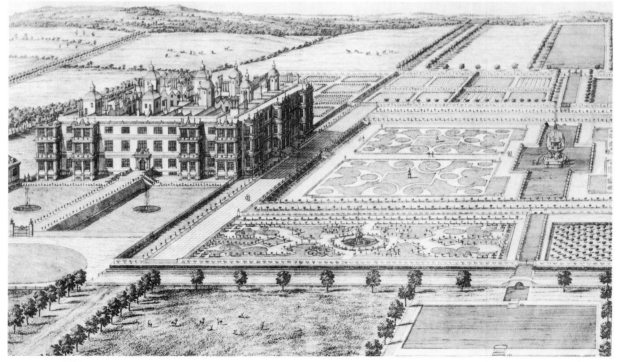

This engraving by Kip shows the formal gardens replaced by Capability Brown's landscaped parkland.

*Apart from the fireplace and minstrels' gallery, the Great
Hall is much as Thynne planned it in 1559.*

Showmanship has continued to be the salvation of
Longleat. In 1964 the impresario Jimmy Chipper-
field suggested the establishment of a 'safari park',
an unheard of proposal in its day. Despite oppo-
sition levied both locally and nationally (his peers
sternly adjured him that a Wiltshireman should
stick to cattle, sheep and deer) the Marquess adopted the idea with such success that 'The Lions of
Longleat' became a household phrase. The stately
home industry had been born in a slightly bewil-
dered post-war world. Longleat has maintained an
unabashedly populist approach, appealing to the
well-known British tendency to love a lord. Lions,
hippos and steam engines exist alongside this splendid Elizabethan-fronted house with its sumptuous
interiors. The portrait of the Marquess shows him
not only as owner but as enthusiastic promoter.

It is, perhaps, appropriate that Longleat should
have been the first to blaze the tourist trail to
solvency, for it was the first of the Elizabethan
prodigy houses. Its builder was a Midlander, John
Thynne, who was born in Shropshire of humble
parentage. A self-educated, self-made man, hard
and thrusting, his portrait at Longleat shows him
characteristically clutching a sword. But though he

was undoubtedly physically courageous, gaining his
knighthood on the battlefield of Pinkie in Scotland,
it was not as a fighter that he made his money, but as
a manipulator and fixer. He was steward to the first
Duke of Somerset, Protector and virtually ruler of
England during the minority of Edward VI. Thynne
nearly shared Somerset's fate but where the master
lost his head on Tower Hill, the steward was merely
fined £2,000 – a fate which for Thynne was scarcely
preferable to death.

His house became his central passion. In 1540 he
had bought the remains of an Augustinian priory in
Wiltshire for £53, and began building about seven
years later. Work continued for twenty years, but
scarcely had the house been completed when most
of it was destroyed by fire. Doggedly, Thynne began
again and produced one of the paradoxes of architectural history. Although he had two well-known
architects on his pay-roll, the Englishman Robert
Smythson and a Frenchman, Allen Maynard, the
overall impress of the house emanated from him.
And this brutal, unsubtle, penny-pinching par-
venue, like Bess of Hardwick, transcended his day;
influenced by the new tide of thought that was
sweeping northward from Italy, he created one of
the first truly Renaissance houses in England.

Externally, Thynne's house looked much as it
does today, with its skyline of graceful little turrets,
some of which are the intimate banqueting houses of

*Longleat's ceilings are its great glory. A detail from the
saloon, inspired by the Palazzo Massimo, Rome.*

One of the earliest, and finest examples of the Elizabethan prodigy house, Longleat introduced the Italianate style into England.

the period. Inside, the Great Hall is also detectably his, from the flagstones to the roof. But elsewhere all is changed. In 1757 Capability Brown transformed the formal water gardens, created from the millstream of the priory – the original Long Leat – into a series of lakes. The story of the house followed that familiar graph of rise, fall and, occasional rise that characterizes the history of great houses. In the eighteenth century, Longleat was neglected for fifteen years. In the nineteenth century, its interior was totally altered by the fourth Marquess who, returning from his Grand Tour with a passion for all things Italian, and with his coffers full from the agricultural boom of the mid-century, threw himself into the task of redecorating without thought of cost. The ceiling of the State Dining Room is composed not simply of decorations of the Italian school, but actual Italian paintings painstakingly inserted into the ceiling. And despite its modest name, the ceiling of the Breakfast Room is copied from the Doge's Palace in Venice, as, too, is the ceiling of the Lower Dining Room. The sumptuous style of decoration was carried out by Italian craftsmen under the direction of John Crace in the 1860s.

The twentieth century is reflected in the remarkable murals of Alexander Thynne, Lord Weymouth and heir to Longleat. Among much else, he has proclaimed the independent State of Wessex with Longleat as its capital, and announced his disapproval of hereditary titles. Having studied as an artist, he has covered the walls of his private apartments with enormous murals created out of sawdust and household paints. They include illustrations of the Kama Sutra and the Paranoia Murals. Not surprisingly, perhaps, they do not feature in the official guide, but a separate publication by Lord Weymouth, which also includes an account of his philosophy and artistic techniques, is available.

BURGHLEY HOUSE, NORTHAMPTONSHIRE

1 mile (1.6 km) SE of Stamford, just off A1

WILLIAM Cecil, Lord Burghley, lies not far from his great house under an ornate tomb in the church of St Martin, Stamford, where he was laid to rest in 1598. The funeral ceremony was in Westminster Abbey but at his own request he was brought, without pomp, to his house and then buried in the town where he had started his career. That career was an object lesson in the fact that the best way to make money in Tudor England was to be a lawyer. Historians have had some harsh things to say about Burghley: the merciless manner in which he harried Roman Catholics; the cold skill with which he jockeyed Mary, Queen of Scots, to her death. But Queen Elizabeth used him as a staff to support and chastise. In his personal life he emerges as a warm human being, never so happy, it was said 'as when he could get his table set around with young little children. He was happy in most worldly things, but

most happy in his children'. There are worse epitaphs.

Cecil began building in 1556 on the remains of a monastery known as Burghe. Writing to his friend Sir Christopher Hatton, who was also engaged in building a vast house at Holdenby, Cecil gives some indication of the motivation behind these monstrous buildings that were springing up over England. They were designed to impress the queen, tempting her to a visit which, though financially expensive, was politically desirable. 'God send us both long to enjoy her,' Cecil wrote, 'for we both mean to expend our purse in these.' He succeeded in his purpose but poor Hatton did not: Elizabeth never came near Holdenby.

Cecil appears to have acted as his own architect, and the house was largely finished by his death in 1598. Daniel Defoe's description of its external appearance in 1722 holds good today. 'It was more like a town than a house,' he thought. 'The towers and the pinnacles, so high and placed at such a distance from one another, look like so many distant parish churches in a town.' But the interior had already changed greatly. Cecil's descendant, the fifth Earl of Exeter, was a dedicated traveller and a passionate admirer of Italian culture, and in 1680 began to turn the austere Elizabethan rooms into the modish Baroque. The fashionable Neapolitan painter, Antonio Verrio, was installed – and proved to be an expensive burden. For ten years he lived sumptuously and autocratically, bringing in his own servants, relatives and friends to form a miniature court and his patron was heartily glad to see the back of him. But he brought fame to the house.

Celia Fiennes visited it shortly before Defoe, giving a more detailed picture of the interior, in particular of Verrio's recently completed murals. Although impressed, as a strong-minded Puritan lady she deplored the large visible expanses of opulent female flesh. Burghley 'was very fine in pictures, but they were all without Garments or very little that was the only fault the immodesty of the pictures especially in my lord's apartment'. But she was fascinated with everything else, the great gate by Tijou in particular. 'The door you enter is of iron carved the finest I ever saw, all sorts of leaves

The old-fashioned courtyard, showing its rather claustrophobic, but essentially private nature. The stone is in fine condition after four centuries.

The Heaven Room, not only Verrio's undoubted masterpiece, but probably the finest painted room in England, completed in 1694.

Burghley's splendid roofscape. Tijou's gate, which so fascinated Celia Fiennes, is in the centre of the range.

flowers figures birds beasts wheate in the Carving', and she calculated that it took at least two hours to see the house, much the same as it does today.

Verrio's work is the showpiece of the house, in particular the extraordinary Heaven Room. Although three walls and the ceiling are totally covered with mythological figures (some of which stride out disconcertingly, or peer over the spectator's shoulder at eye level) the room is bright and welcoming, largely because the fourth wall is almost entirely glass. Verrio put himself in the picture, a plump, balding man looking decidedly pleased with himself, as well he might considering how agreeably he lived while creating this fantasy.

In the early 1980s Burghley House encountered the crisis only too common among these great houses. The Marquess of Exeter died in October 1981 (the title going to a brother in Canada) and his wife died the following June. There was no-one to take responsibility for the house. The Trustees then approached Lady Victoria Leatham, the Marquess's daughter by his second marriage. She and her husband were living elsewhere, pursuing demanding, full-time careers. A building of this nature makes voracious demands on time; although it was in good condition – indeed, to stand in the courtyard is to be amazed by the quality of the stonework – parts of it were undeniably shabby and the logistics of the whole formidable. The kitchen is 200 yards from the living quarters! But they decided in favour, moved in at the end of 1982 and began the task of adapting the vast treasure chest to its present dual role of family house and public heritage.

For it is a treasure house. In April 1983 a remarkable exhibition of Oriental and European ceramics, comprising some 250 pieces, was put on display, all of which were found in the house – some pieces tucked away in long forgotten cupboards. They include rare Japanese ceramics acquired by the fifth Earl during his Grand Tour, and faithfully recorded by his private secretary, Culpepper Tanner, in a detailed inventory. The inventory not only survives, but proved vital in tracking down and assembling the items in the exhibition.

MAPLEDURHAM HOUSE, OXFORDSHIRE

4 miles NW of Reading
off Caversham-Woodcote road (A4074)

IF Mapledurham House seems oddly familiar to devotees of *The Wind in the Willows*, there is a simple explanation. E.H. Shepherd, the most successful illustrator of this children's classic, probably used the house as his model for Toad Hall. Kenneth Grahame, the author, lived just across the river at Pangbourne and knew this stretch of the Thames intimately.

Mapledurham is more than a house; it is a tiny working model of a complete feudal estate, with almshouses, mill, church, Big House and estate cottages, miraculously surviving in unspoiled Oxfordshire hills almost on the fringes of the ugly sprawl of Reading. Access to Mapledurham is either over Caversham Bridge, or by boat, or the long way round through Pangbourne, across the toll-bridge into Whitchurch and then down a long rough road. Nobody casually passes through the tiny village – one makes a pilgrimage to it.

On approaching the house from this land side, it is noticeable that one of the little window gables seems to be glistening even on a dull day. For it is covered with oyster shells, the once secret sign that this was a safe house for Roman Catholics. It has always been a Catholic house, holding fast to the Old Faith even during the fiercest years of persecution.

The house seems to be turning its back to the visitor. Sir Michael Blount, who built it in the year of the Armada, deliberately turned it to face the east, bearing in mind the warning of the fashionable physician, Andrew Boorde: 'the south wynde doth corrupt and doth make evyl vapours'. Like all living houses, Mapledurham has adjusted, adapted and fidgeted itself into comfort over the centuries, but it is still a late Elizabethan house. The modern entrance is through what used to be the Great Hall, remodelled in 1828 to make an entrance hall but still with the dignity of its origins. A delightful feature is a series of carved animal heads, some of them portraying a proverb or fable like the extraordinary

The east front of Mapledurham, probably the model for E. H. Shepherd's Toad Hall in The Wind in the Willows.

The family built their chapel in 1797, taking advantage of the Catholic Relief Act which had been passed in 1791.

four-eared, four-eyed creature illustrating Aesop's story of the wolf in sheep's clothing. Flanking the fireplace are two deer, carved from a single tree.

Visitors are usually taken next into the Library where there are portraits of Teresa and Martha Blount, the close friends of Alexander Pope. He penned for Teresa a teasing little poem, commiserating with her on leaving the bustling life of town for the dullness of the countryside:

> To morning walks and prayers three hours a day
> To muse and spill her solitary Tea
> Or o'er cold coffee trifle with a spoon
> Count the clock slow and dine exact at noon.

Nevertheless Pope himself was a frequent visitor to the house between 1707 and 1715, and his portrait by Kneller and some of his possessions are preserved upstairs in the boudoir.

Mapledurham experienced the common fate of so many country houses, passing into the hands of a collateral branch of the family, declining almost into extinction and then slowly being brought to life again by a devoted owner. After World War II it was all but derelict when John Eyston, the present owner, in 1960 persuaded the Historic Buildings

Councils to make a grant and so began a long, slow programme of restoration.

The restoration was not limited to the house. Close by is the beautiful watermill, 100 years older than the house itself, and which was actually working until 1947 when it became totally derelict. Now in working order, it is possible to buy flour from one of the very last working watermills in the country.

The entrance hall was built in 1828, incorporating the Tudor Great Hall.

LAYER MARNEY TOWER, ESSEX

3 miles (6.4 km) from Tiptree,
1 mile (1.6 km) s of B1022 Colchester-Maldon road

IN terms of modern skyscrapers – or even of medieval cathedrals – Layer Marney Tower is not particularly high, being little over eighty feet. But its total unexpectedness in the flat Essex countryside, and the fact that it is flanked by relatively low domestic buildings gives it a presence out of all proportion to its actual size.

Henry, first Lord Marney, who built the tower about 1520, doubtless intended it to be simply the gatehouse to a far grander edifice than now exists. But with his death in 1523, and that of his son two years later, the short-lived barony became extinct.

Lord Marney had been a Privy Councillor to Henry VIII and almost certainly accompanied him to the fabulous Field of the Cloth of Gold. Like his contemporary, Sir Richard Weston of Sutton Place, he was undoubtedly influenced by the new Italian style of architecture that was entering France. Terracotta was one of the features of this style and, again like Sir Richard, he used it when designing his own house. The windows, in particular, of Layer Marney and Sutton Place bear a family resemblance.

The lavish use of glass on the tower betrays its purpose: it was built for prestige, not defence. A number of these tower houses were springing up all over England during the fifteenth and early sixteenth centuries, East Anglia being particularly rich in them. Sir Henry was almost certainly seeking to outdo his son-in-law, Sir Edmond Bedingfield, whose great gatehouse tower at Oxburgh was one of the wonders of Norfolk, and Sir Henry succeeded.

The terracotta tiles at Layer Marney illustrate its affinity with Sutton Place.

The hall, looking much as it would have done at the time of Lord Marney's death in 1523.

The outstanding size of the gatehouse implies that Lord Marney intended the house itself to be a far larger building.

LOSELEY HOUSE, SURREY

2½ miles (4 km) sw of Guildford,
1½ miles (2.1 km) n of Godalming (off A3100)

LOSELEY House came into being indirectly as a result of that great sixteenth-century act of plunder, the dissolution of the monasteries. When, in 1562, Sir William More decided to rebuild his old manor house in a style fit to welcome his pernickety queen, Elizabeth I, he found in the abandoned Cistercian monastery of Waverley Abbey a ready-made source of worked stone. The blocks which his masons carted away were at least 450 years old, so his house was mellow with age even as it rose. They used clunch to dress the corners, obtaining it from the vast chalk quarries of Guildford some three miles away. This soft, indigenous material was also used with great effect for interior decoration. The extra-

ordinary chimney-piece in the Drawing Room now looks as pristine as the day it was carved from a single block of chalk four centuries ago.

The Mores were not often in the dangerous mainstream of history. For over 400 years the family quietly farmed their rich fields and meadows – no sequesterings, no assassinations, no beheadings, only the occasional domestic tempest. The family records, now in the county muniments, survive to give substance to their story. In them, Lord Burghley warns his friend Sir Christopher More that the Queen is intent on visiting Loseley and the entertainment had better be up to standard. The Earl of Southampton, a 'suspected Papist', is tem-

Most of the building materials for Loseley came from the ruins of Waverley Abbey, near Farnham, giving the house an instantly mature appearance.

The chimney piece in the drawing room is unique, carved out of a single block of chalk to a Holbein design. The ceiling was decorated for the visit of James I.

porarily placed in the custody of Sir William More with consequent dislocation of family life. Anne, the daughter of Sir George More, secretly marries John Donne and her infuriated father throws the presumptious poet into the Fleet prison for his pains.

In 1689 the house passed by marriage to the Molyneux family, now called More-Molyneux but still living in the same house as country gentlemen and farmers. The twentieth century took its toll. When the present owner, James More-Molyneux, inherited it in 1945, he and his wife faced an all but impossible task. The roof leaked; the windows were broken; horses were grazing on the once velvet lawns and grass now grew up to the windowsills.

But Loseley sought, and eventually found its twentieth-century salvation in the oldest of all sources of wealth – the land. A herd of Jersey cows was built up, and the estate almost accidentally developed a flourishing business in dairy produce. 'The farm secretary at the estate office said it was a pity to throw all the skimmed milk away. Couldn't we make cottage cheese? So we did. Then yoghurt.' Eventually the estate entered into an association with an expanding chain of health-food shops. They have also created a successful trade making prefabricated houses, which began with the casting of concrete blocks for the estate. Today their houses are sold throughout the world.

The estate consists of 1,000 acres comprised of six farms all busily working in an area often pejoratively dismissed as 'commuter country'. Farm tours now form one of its many attractions, and in season, fruit picking attracts hundreds of visitors. But Loseley House is still essentially a family home, little changed over the centuries. No great access of wealth in the eighteenth or nineteenth centuries tempted its owners to pull down and rebuild in the fashionable style. Passing through the doorway with its welcoming motto, *Invidiae claudor, pateo sed semper amico* (Closed to envy, always open to a friend) is to become aware of a present maintaining close contact with its past.

HATFIELD HOUSE, HERTFORDSHIRE

In Hatfield, 21 miles (33.7 km) N of London

TWENTIETH-CENTURY town planning – in particular, the creation of an immense new road system – has buried Hatfield in a vast, anonymous urban development. It is only too easy to go speeding past, unaware of the delightful little market town that still exists, attached to this enormous palace that covers almost as great an area. But it is worth threading a way through the modern overlay and entering Hatfield House from the town side rather than by the great ceremonial drive, for that way one proceeds chronologically from the older to the newer part of the building. 'New' here is of course relative, for the house was built in 1611 by the son of the same Lord Burghley who built Burghley House in Northamptonshire.

Climbing a steep hill, lined with elegant Georgian houses, one enters a massive gatehouse. Immediately opposite is a great red brick building, the remains of a palace built by Cardinal Morton in 1497. It became the childhood home – and subsequently the prison – of the young princess who became known to history as Elizabeth I. Her half-sister, Mary, had also known the house as a prison. Legend has it that she hastened to the top of the tower to see her father, Henry VIII, ride by and called out to him but he did not acknowledge her presence by the flicker of an eyebrow.

The tower remains, and so does the Great Hall, but everything else was demolished by Robert Cecil. Hatfield was, in effect, forced upon him. His father, that great builder, was also the founder of a house called Theobalds in Hertfordshire and left it to him in his will. James I much admired it, and 'suggested' to Cecil that he should exchange it for one of the King's own mansions at Hatfield, not far away. Emanating from such a source this proposal was tantamount to a command and Cecil, with what grace he could muster, took over Morton's old mansion in 1607. He demolished most of it, using the bricks to build his own house. He apparently

The south front of Hatfield House. Built to the formal E plan, it was the work of Robert Cecil, in 1611.

Much of the chapel was remodelled in the 19th century but these windows are those installed by Robert Cecil.

The Marble Hall at Hatfield is the last and most elaborate version of the medieval Great Hall.

The Grand Staircase, with its 'dog gates', is the English version, in oak, of the fashionable Renaissance style.

The 1st Marchioness of Salisbury by Sir Joshua Reynolds.

acted as architect himself, though Inigo Jones laid out the splendid stone forecourt and a young carpenter, Robert Lyminge, was to learn enough of his trade here to emerge as architect at Blickling eight years later.

The enormous building had one primary function – to entice the monarch to a visit. Built in the newly fashionable 'compact' form, that is, without a courtyard, its two great wings were designed to act as lodgings for the king and queen, the king to the east, the queen to the west. The rest of the Cecil household was tucked away in lesser quarters. An inventory of 1611 among the Hatfield papers makes it clear that two sets of furniture were provided for the royal lodgings, one for use by the king and queen and a less valuable set for use in their absence. Ironically, James I never visited Hatfield in full state.

LITTLE MORETON HALL, CHESHIRE

4 miles sw of Congleton, off A34
The National Trust

THE first sight of this dramatic black and white building is doubly misleading. It seems remarkably unstable, with the upper storey leaning over at all angles, and looks as though it was built all at the same period. But wood, its primary material, has a trick of settling in on itself, of moving in dozens of ways to snug itself down for the centuries. And the building of Moreton Hall spanned well over 120 years but, because the same beautiful material was used throughout, it seems homogenous.

The only approach to the house is the bridge over the moat that completely surrounds it. Here, one encounters immediately one of those profound differences of value that separate one historical period from another. Immediately to the left of this unique and ceremonial entrance is the point of

discharge of two major privies – an unthinkable arrangement in a twentieth-century building, but accepted quite casually by the sixteenth century.

The house grew in a clockwise manner, creating a courtyard at its heart. The oldest part is the northern range, opposite the gatehouse. Here is the Great Hall – literally so, for when it was built in 1480 it completely dominated the rest of the house, which then appeared simply as an appendage to it. A century later, this towering chamber lost its attraction to the family and it was divided horizontally. But some time before 1807, when John Sell Cotman sketched the Hall much as it appears today, the floor was removed – part of the restless adapting, and readapting which marks all living houses. The ghostly outlines of the doors that were made in the

The courtyard of Little Moreton Hall. The lantern windows were added to the earlier north wing in 1559.

The proud boast of Richard Dale who 'made thies windovs by the grac of God' in 1559.

upper half of the walls are still visible under the whitewash.

Some sixty years after the Great Hall was built, bays were added to it and the neighbouring withdrawing room, initiating a period of expansion that was to continue until 1600. A succession of buildings crept down the eastern side, and then turned west to create the gatehouse range. And it was on this range that the family seems to have been touched by megalomania. No Elizabethan gentleman's house could be deemed complete without its Long Gallery, where he could stroll during inclement weather and, perhaps, hang a few portraits of his ancestors. John Moreton decided that the only place for this fashionable addition was balanced on the top of the southern, or gatehouse range. The nature of the architectural problems posed is vividly demonstrated by the great beams of

The north front, dating from the fifteenth century, faces the Elizabethan-style garden laid out in recent years.

the gallery's roof: they are quite evidently holding the walls together like great clamps.

Apart from the black and white woodwork, the most characteristic feature of Little Moreton Hall is its glass windows. Glass was no longer quite the luxury it had been a century before when cautious owners took their glass windows with them from manor to manor. By 1559 when Richard Dale, a carpenter, put up a series of windows and proudly recorded the fact on the lintel, there were over a dozen glass factories working in England. What is unusual is the variety of patterns used throughout the house.

The impression carried away from the Hall, unlike that conveyed by so many houses of the period, is of an interior flooded with light. The Long Gallery is particularly favoured with windows along the length of every wall. The house is almost completely empty today, which enables the visitor

Placed precariously above the south wing, the Long Gallery is clamped together by the roof beams.

The south wing of Little Moreton Hall, seen across the moat. The Long Gallery runs behind the strip window on the top floor.

to appreciate to the full the virtuosity of three or four generations of carpenters. But the emptiness does not detract from the feeling that this was once a home: to the contrary, there is an almost eerie sensation of having arrived at an interim period, that one family has moved out and another is just about to move in.

The Moretons (who took their name from a local farmstead) were associated with the place from the thirteenth to the twentieth century. The last private owner, Bishop Thomas Abraham, was a cousin of the family who inherited it in 1913. He left a vivid description of the house as he first saw it in 1892. 'I remember taking a day off at Lichfield to run down and see what she [his cousin, Elizabeth Moreton] had left me and shall not forget the thrill as I topped the rise after Scholar Green, walking from Kidsgrive Station, and saw the front of the old black and white house in spring sunshine confronting me. It has been in my heart and dreams ever since.' Bishop Moreton did much to preserve the Hall before giving it to the National Trust in 1937.

HEVER CASTLE, KENT

3 miles (4.8 km) SE of Edenbridge off B2026

HEVER has three totally different claims to historic interest. It was here, sometime in the 1520s, that Henry VIII met Anne Boleyn, and the course of English history began to change. In 1903, the American millionaire, William Waldorf Astor, bought the decrepit building and created one of the most brilliant of architectural restorations. But in 1982 the present Lord Astor, descendant of William, decided that life in the castle, shared with a quarter of a million visitors, was insupportable, and placed it on the open market. A property company acquired it and, after breaking up the vast estate, turned the ancient edifice into a purely tourist attraction.

After the Boleyns, or Bullens, had died out, the castle deteriorated and by the late nineteenth century was simply a farmhouse. Built in the mid-fourteenth century, the very nature of the exquisite building dictated the remarkable solution which Astor adopted in order to make it a family home again. The castle is entirely surrounded by a moat and, as with most buildings of its type, the accommodation available was scarcely up to modern standards – certainly not the standards of a millionaire with a vast staff and wide social contacts. To have extended the actual castle would have been to destroy the very characteristics which attracted Astor – in particular, the moat. He therefore decided simply to restore the castle itself, and build a totally separate structure for domestic purposes. That separate structure took the form of a Tudor 'village'. From a distance, particularly when viewed from the castle, its variegated materials and skylines have all the appearance of a village that has evolved over the

The 'village' to the left of the castle – Astor's imaginative solution to the accommodation problem – is in fact one huge interconnected building.

The castle set in its moat. Apart from access to the village, the only entrance is still by medieval drawbridge.

centuries. But though it appears to be composed of a dozen or more separate elements it is, in fact, one vast building, all of whose parts are connected, and joined to the castle itself by a bridge. Over a thousand men worked for four years on this creation, laying out the beautiful gardens, and restoring the castle.

The standard of restoration and workmanship would have been outstanding even for the 1980s; for its day it is little less than extraordinary. The attention to detail can perhaps best be illustrated by Henry VIII's lock, an elaborate mechanism that always travelled with the monarch, and was placed on the door of every room in which he slept. Astor not only acquired it, but had an exact copy made, the two being used for the doors in the sombre dining room. It takes an expert of great skill to detect which is the original and which is the copy.

The castle was stripped bare when Astor acquired it, giving him a free hand not only to restore and decorate according to sixteenth-century taste but also to hang paintings and tapestries that illuminate its major period, Tudor. This careful choice of objects seem now to belong to this building and no other: Holbein's portraits of Anne Boleyn and her royal murderer; the poignant layette for Queen Mary's baby that was never born and Gheeraerts' portrait of an acidic Queen Elizabeth are among the treasures that add a priceless dimension to this ancient castle.

King Henry VIII's lock.

HARDWICK HALL, DERBYSHIRE

2 miles (3.2 km) S of Chesterfield-Mansfield road (A617),
6½ miles (10.4 km) NW of Mansfield
and 9½ miles (13.6 km) SE of Chesterfield
The National Trust

BESS of Hardwick lies alone on her splendid tomb in Derby cathedral, crowned with a coronet, an altogether appropriate monument. Which of her four husbands could be chosen to lie in effigy beside her, and who could doubt her right to that circlet of sovereignty, queen as she was over a sizeable area of Derbyshire? Her portrait as an old woman in Hardwick Hall itself gives further substance to her character. One is immediately reminded of that other Bess, her contemporary Elizabeth, Queen of England – except that Bess of Hardwick is, if anything, rather more regal. The great beaked nose, the firm mouth with compressed lips, the cold, dark eyes under supercilious brows all attest to the character of a woman who, in her seventies, expressed her will in brick and stone in the form of one of the most extraordinary of Tudor houses.

The splendid staircase which leads to the equally impressive High Great Chamber, Bess's 'presence chamber'.

The year of her birth is uncertain, but was probably around 1520. Her family was solid, rather than distinguished, owning a manor house among the Derbyshire hills. Her first marriage, at the age of fifteen, was to a local squire named Barlow, who died soon afterwards, leaving her a sizeable fortune. Her own mistress now, and no longer simply the matrimonial pawn of her parents, she could afford to wait nearly fifteen years for her second husband. Sir William Cavendish was a great catch, for he was a man who was not only in the confidence of the king but, as Treasurer of the Chamber, had access to that vast flood of wealth brought about by the dissolution of the monasteries. His political strength lay in the south (the Cavendishes originated in Suffolk) but Bess wanted to remain on her own ground.

Even today, Derbyshire is a little England of its own: in winter, snowfalls can cut off entire towns for days. In the sixteenth century it was as remote as Scotland. Nevertheless, Cavendish acquiesced in his bride's wishes. They bought a manor house called Chatsworth and immediately began rebuilding it in a grander manner. Cavendish died, leaving Bess in possession of his vast properties, including the now splendid Chatsworth. One more marriage, to an otherwise unknown man called William St Loe who died in 1565 (leaving her yet more estates) prepared her for the biggest catch of all. In 1568 she married George Talbot, sixth Earl of Shrewsbury, one of the most powerful men in England. Dynastic marriages were not often happy but this one proved unusually acrimonious – a fact which led directly to the creation of Hardwick Hall. Before long, the quarrels between Earl and Countess were so violent that she moved out of Chatsworth, back to the family home. But what had been adequate for young Bess of Hardwick was decidedly not good enough for the Countess of Shrewsbury. Talbot's death left her in sole possession of an enormous fortune and, at the age of seventy, she threw herself into creating the biggest house of its day.

Although Bess employed an architect, Robert Smythson, one may be certain that this is, in every

Bess of Hardwick's initials flamboyantly crown her towering house with its remarkable range of windows – 'more glass than wall'.

and Hardwick, passed the latter over to the Treasury as part payment of death duties. The 400-year-old link was broken, but the future of the house assured for it was given to the National Trust.

Of all places in the house, Bess of Hardwick lives on in that splendidly named room, the High Great Chamber, used purely for ceremonial purposes. Placed on the second floor, the chamber provided the pretext for a grand ceremonial staircase. And Bess grasped that pretext. The great stone stairs at Hardwick seem like a frozen cascade. It was in the High Great Chamber that Bess held those masques and entertainments beloved of the Elizabethans. Given so bizarre a character, one might expect the room to be a blaze of gaudy colour but the overall effect is of muted browns and greys. The room was built around the tapestries that cover the walls for they were bought in 1587, four years before the house was begun: they fit just below, and are echoed by the painted plasterwork frieze. The room is austerely furnished: Farthingale chairs stand stiffly around the wall in the Elizabethan manner, and there is a walnut table that sums up Bess of Hardwick's marital career for it carries the arms of Hardwick, Cavendish and Talbot.

sense, her house. Like her contemporary, Thynne, at Longleat, this not particularly imaginative woman managed to transcend her day, leaving fashion behind to create what must have seemed a startling innovation. In place of the courtyard, that dull claustrophobic space that was derived from the cloisters, she used the modern H formula, creating a solid compact building. The hall, instead of running parallel to the front in the medieval manner, is at right angles to it and towers up through two storeys. But it was in her use of glass that she set her impress upon the house. The main west front, crowned with the proud initials ES and a coronet, is a glitter of reflection, the stonework used simply as a frame for windows. She, or her architect, cheated: anxious for symmetry at all costs the windows ignore the position of the rooms behind and in some cases the floor actually bisects the windows.

For the visitor, the attraction of the house lies largely in the fact that it looks exactly as it did when its formidable creator breathed her last here at the age of eighty-eight. Her descendants preferred Chatsworth, over the following centuries transforming it from an Elizabethan house to that which we see today. Hardwick they left alone; but it remained in the family and was maintained in good condition. Even Bess's furniture remained *in situ*, as can be seen from the inventory she drew up in her own hand at the age of eighty-four. In 1959, the Duke of Devonshire, inheritor of both Chatsworth

Bess of Hardwick in her widowhood.

The Long Gallery, some 166 feet in length, was probably designed to take

the Flemish tapestry. Bess's portrait still hangs here where she placed it.

RIPLEY CASTLE, NORTH YORKSHIRE

In Ripley; $3\frac{1}{2}$ miles (5.6 km) N of Harrogate,
$7\frac{1}{2}$ miles (12.1 km) from Ripon

IN 1784, Sir John Ingilby of Ripley Castle was faced with a problem common to his class and time: his old manor house was decidedly the worse for wear after some 300 years of continuous occupation. His solution was decidedly uncommon. Where his contemporaries would have happily razed the old house and built completely anew, he recognized the past as something valuable in its own right. As he wrote to a friend, 'I was determined upon preserving as much as possible of the old place and by that means have spoiled my plan in the opinion of some people – but notwithstanding the inconveniences of our Ancestors' buildings I prefer them to the modern structures.' He then added, in a spirit which seems of the twentieth rather than of the eighteenth century, 'Any man who has money can build a house, but few can show the same house his family has lived in for so many years.'

Ripley Castle today is a mosaic of periods, the worn-out swept away and entirely rebuilt (it is now thought by the architect, William Bellwood) but the rest refurbished. The oldest part of the house is the gatehouse, built in 1418. The Crown was most reluctant to allow private citizens the right to build fortifications and the Ingilbys received their permission to do so only because of the threat from the Scots, and those under General 'Black' Douglas in particular.

Ripley Castle seen from the park: an example of a fortified manor house transformed into an elegant residence.

The old tower of 1555 also survives. The ground floor houses the Library and it was here, on a July night in 1644, that the redoubtable Lady Ingilby sat guard over the 'rebel' Oliver Cromwell while armed with two pistols. The battle of Marston Moor had just been fought; her husband Sir William was in hiding near the battlefield when Cromwell arrived at the castle requesting lodging for the night. She agreed reluctantly and led the way to the Library 'where, sitting on a sopha, these two extraordinary personages equally jealous of the other's intention, passed the whole night'. Asked later why she had two pistols, Lady Ingilby answered simply 'I might have missed with the first.' Altogether, it is an episode that does equal honour to the lady and the 'rebel'.

In this same room is a portrait of a member of the family who is currently a candidate for canonization – Francis Ingilby, a Jesuit priest who was hanged, drawn and quartered in 1586. Upstairs in the Knight's Chamber is a tiny priest's hole which Francis probably used while evading capture for nearly four years. So well constructed and hidden is it that it was not discovered until 1964 when repairs were being made to the room. This Knight's Chamber has its original sixteenth-century panelling and with the low ceiling conveys the dark, rather claustrophobic nature that characterizes so much of the domestic architecture of this period. The beautiful Tower Room has a splendid ceiling, especially made to commemorate the visit of James I in 1603, and a curious modern story. During renovations in 1930 the present fireplace at the far end of the room was detected behind the panelling.

The sixteenth-century Tower Room – venue of a poltergeist?

In order to protect the discovery, the room was locked for the night. On being opened in the morning a scene of utter confusion was disclosed, the massive furniture having been tossed around like so much matchwood. The cause is unknown – it has never happened again.

The village attached to the castle is an intriguing example of idiosyncratic town planning. By the early nineteenth century the cottages were in an advanced state of decay and the decision was made to demolish them all and rebuild. The current Ingilby was a decided Francophile and instead of building the village in the vernacular he modelled it on one in Alsace-Lorraine. It is for this reason that the village hall, a solidly built structure, boasts the name 'Hotel de Ville'. The little village does, in fact, have the indefinable air of a township.

And, as a corollary to Sir John Ingilby's devotion to the old house in the eighteenth century, it is worth recording the dedication of the current owner, Sir Thomas. When he came of age he was offered the choice of selling up or shouldering the increasing burden of maintaining the place. He chose the latter, and over the past few years more and more means have been explored to allow the house to contribute to its own maintenance. The use of fuel from the estate for the modern wood-burning equipment that now heats the castle, shows how even the traditional has been redirected to serve new needs.

The Library, where Cromwell was 'entertained'.

SUTTON PLACE, SURREY

2 miles (3.2 km) NW of Guildford, off A1

SUTTON Place gained a certain element of fame in the 1960s and 1970s when it became the home of Paul Getty. He acquired it for the most prosaic of reasons: it was cheaper to buy a 450-year-old house which, though beautiful, nobody wanted, than to pay for hotels. Sutton Place became both his home, and the European headquarters of Getty Oil. It was opened, somewhat grudgingly, to the public on severely limited occasions – the gardens eight times a year and the house itself for a couple of hours on a Sunday afternoon. Two thousand people and more would form an immense crocodile and shuffle through the three principal rooms, though their interest probably lay less in the Tudor mansion than the fact that it was the home of the richest man in the world – and sometimes it was possible to get a glimpse of that fabulous being as he peered out from the gallery.

Getty's death in 1976, and the oil company's subsequent decision to sell the house, posed for Sutton Place the problem that faces so many historic houses. Few private individuals could possibly pay

Francis Bacon's paintings in the sober Great Hall sum up Sutton Place's role as a centre for the arts.

for its upkeep. The State, in the form of local planning officers, resolutely opposed any alterations – yet no large institution could use the house without making drastic alterations to its interior. The Getty regime, by treating the house as a kind of super-luxury hotel for their globe-trotting executives, had provided an answer of sorts. What would happen now that its founder was dead? In due course, a new solution was found.

Sutton Place provides a microcosm of English history. William the Conqueror personally acquired the estate. It was fought over so viciously and damaged so extensively, that in 1353 royal appraisers dismissed it as being virtually valueless. In 1521 Henry VIII gave it to Sir Richard Weston, one of his favourite councillors. Sir Richard may be fairly described as a professional survivor. Despite the fact that his son was beheaded for cuckolding the king (or, to be exact, for contemplating it, the lady in question being Anne Boleyn) Sir Richard remained in high favour. He began to build his house in the mid 1520s.

The archives have been lost and its early history has to be deduced from its appearance. A very early example of the undefended manor house, it is evidence of the builder's confidence in the strength of the monarchy, and the relative tranquility of southern England. (The builders of Norton Conyers, just forty years before, were careful to provide it with good fortifications.) Sutton Place's most obvious characteristic is its Renaissance balance and grace. Weston had spent much time in France (he was among those who accompanied the young Henry to the Field of the Cloth of Gold in 1520) and had been much impressed with the new Italianate chateaux on the Loire.

He built his splendid new house in brick, but liberally ornamented it with terracotta tiles, creating an exotic effect among the Surrey water meadows. They allowed the unknown architect a remarkable degree of precision and plasticity while providing a clue to the parentage of the house: their design is Italian, but their usage English.

The house was originally a quadrangle but fire destroyed one of the ranges. In 1782 the owner, John Webbe-Weston conceived the unnerving idea

The Italianate Loire chateaux may have influenced Sir William Weston when he built Sutton Place.

of cladding the entire fabric of the house in the fashionable stucco classicisms and gothicisms of the period. Fortunately, he was dissuaded. Sutton Place is a testimony to the fact that the best safeguard for a historic building is a decent penury. The family who occupied it never grew rich enough to be able to 'improve' it, and today it is basically the same building as envisaged by Sir Richard Weston.

History repeated itself for Sutton Place. After Getty's death, it was bought in 1979 by the Anglo-Texan Oil Company, who leased it to Stanley J. Seeger. His first intention was to use it as a private home, but gradually the idea evolved of creating a trust, under whose aegis would be attempted the renaissance of an English country house. It was an idea that only a millionaire – and a philanthropic millionaire – could have carried out.

With a paying public limited to around forty at a time, the house and grounds continue to be the main attraction, but in addition there is the permanent Seeger Collection of paintings as well as concerts and visiting exhibitions. Over some eighteen months, 300 people worked on the place at an overall cost of some £5 million. The project for the house was largely restorative, but the development of the garden was entirely creative, the work of Sir Geoffrey Jellicoe, and on a scale unknown since the gardens were designed at Chatsworth. Those who

had wondered how Repton or Capability Brown were able to look into the future and plan their slow-growing miracles could gain an insight by visiting Sutton Place during this formative period. One of the features planned has been a ceremonial avenue of oak trees, which will not achieve maturity for at least another 100 years. A vast lake has been created, together with 'surrealist' gardens where perspective has been doctored. One was inspired by Magritte, another by Miro and a third acts as the setting for Ben Nicolson's vast sculptured wall. This formal garden is perhaps most memorable of all, only the immaturity of the slower-growing plants betraying the fact that it is a recent creation. It looks as though the house had been waiting four and half centuries for this to complete it.

A detail of the outstanding terracotta tiles. Other designs include a visual pun on the name 'Weston'.

DEENE PARK, NORTHAMPTONSHIRE

8 miles (12.8 km) NW of Oundle,
6 miles (9.6 km) NE of Corby on A43

WHEN James Thomas Brudenell, seventh Earl of Cardigan, began the canter that developed into the Charge of the Light Brigade at Balaclava, he was heard to mutter to himself, 'Well, here goes the last of the Brudenells.' Time proved him wrong: 130 years later Brudenells still live in the large house from which he set out on the road to the Crimea, as they have done for the past four centuries or so.

Deene Park perfectly illustrates the English love of understatement, their preference for imprecision of language, for in any European country this 'house' would be classed as a palace. Sir Robert Brudenell, Chief Justice of England, bought it in 1514. He had to pay a ground rent of £18 a year to Westminster Abbey. (And so did his successors. They had to pay that same £18 a year until 1970 when the Church Commissioners sold it to them outright!) A lawyer with the right connections was in a good position for making money, and arranging good marriages for his children. Sir Robert did both, laying the foundation of the Brudenell fortune.

His grandson, Sir Edmund, married an heiress and with her money began building on a grand scale. Legend has it that her life was made so miserable over demands for funds that Sir Edmund's

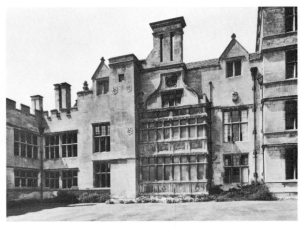

The complex east front, most interesting of all as it probably incorporates the main building of the medieval manor.

conscience-stricken ghost haunts their bedroom. Sir Edmund, in effect, began a building programme that was to continue for nearly 300 years: the last major addition was built in 1810, and as late as 1919 the beautiful little Oak Parlour was enriched with seventeenth-century oak panelling taken from a house on the family's Yorkshire estate.

But Deene Park, like so many of its peers, soon seemed bound for extinction. In World War II it was commandeered for troops and was all but derelict by the end of the 1940s. The family grimly held on in a house with little plumbing, no heating or electricity, a leaking roof, and a kitchen so far from the living area that Mrs Brudenell used a bicycle to reach it. But a generation's devoted work has since restored the house to a living home.

Although the architecture of Deene Park covers nearly three centuries, the visitor is immediately plunged into the Elizabethan heart of the place. The entrance is through a beautiful, dignified courtyard, on one side of which is Sir Edmund's Great Hall, built in 1572, a chamber which combines majesty and homeliness to a remarkable degree. The complex ceiling of carved chestnut soars high up into the gloom, but warmly upholstered couches by the great fireplace show that this is a family house. Next to them is a sixteenth-century refectory table and

The architecture of Deene Park spans nearly three centuries. This beautiful courtyard shows the original Elizabethan hall range, which was built in 1572.

View of the house from across the canal. The bridge was built in the 18th century from the balusters of a 17th-century garden terrace.

bench which, though antique (they have been in the hall since it was built) look as though they were used that morning.

Family portraits are scattered throughout the house, together with those of long-serving members of the staff painted by Richard Foster in 1970. It is impossible to escape the family's most famous, or, at least, most notorious and certainly vainest member, Lord Cardigan. In the Dining Room is de Prades' great painting of him leading the Charge at Balaclava on his chestnut horse, Ronald – Ronald's head and tail are preserved in a case along with the Earl's gaudy uniform. Nearby is James Sant's painting of Lord Cardigan describing the battle to the Royal family. It is said that Queen Victoria was once part of the portrait, but indignantly had herself removed on hearing of Cardigan's private life. An x-ray examination has, alas, punctured another good story, for no trace remains.

The Great Hall, built by Sir Edmund Brudenell in 1572.

THE SEVENTEENTH CENTURY

WILTON HOUSE, WILTSHIRE

In Wilton, 2½ miles (4 km) w of Salisbury on
Exeter road (A30)

At least one detail of Wilton House will be known by name to most visitors, and that is the splendid Double Cube room, designed by Inigo Jones and completed by John Webb about 1653. At once majestic and elegant with its high, rich ceiling, and white painted walls with gilded decorations, it was planned as a setting for Van Dyke's superb series of family portraits. Improbably, this most famous of English seventeenth-century interiors was the oper- ations room for Army Southern Command during World War II. One can only postulate the decision of an anti-Arts Minister to create so bizarre a set of circumstances. But the room and the house both survived, and Wilton House today holds probably the richest art collection still in private hands.

William Herbert, first Earl of Pembroke, founded the family fortune. This voluble Welshman was already high in royal favour when he married Anne

The sober, almost austere exterior does little to prepare the visitor for the interior richness of colour.

The Double Cube Room, perhaps the most famous feature of the house. Designed by Inigo Jones and completed by Webb about 1653, it appears today exactly as it was when built.

The Colonnade Room, formerly the State Bedroom, decorated in white and gold. Completed in the early 17th century, most of the furniture is 18th century, by William Kent.

The Library, 'ungothicised' by Reginald, 15th Earl of Pembroke, who succeeded to the title in 1913.

Palladian Bridge, built in 1737 by Henry, 9th Earl and Roger Morris.

Parr, sister of Henry VIII's sixth and last wife, in 1534. Henry, with his customary generosity with other people's property, gave him the abbey of Wilton in 1544 and he immediately began to build the present Tudor house. Tradition has it that he sought the advice of the King's brilliant painter, Hans Holbein.

It was in his son's day that Wilton House became a celebrated centre of politics and the arts, somewhat resembling the role that Cliveden was to play three centuries later. Henry, second Earl of Pembroke, was married to Mary Sidney, brother of the poet and soldier Sir Philip Sidney. 'In her time', said the gossip John Aubrey 'Wilton House was like a college, there were so many learned and ingeniose persons. She was the greatest patroness of wit and learning of her time.' Among those who thronged her court were naturally her brother Philip (scenes from his *Arcadia* are to be found in the Single Cube Room) Ben Jonson, Edmund Spenser, and Philip Massinger, and there is a strong, though unsubstantiated tradition that Shakespeare, with his company, gave a first performance at Wilton of one of his comedies – possibly *As You Like It*.

BLICKLING HALL, NORFOLK

$1\frac{1}{2}$ miles (2.4 km) NW of Aylsham on N side of B1354,
15 miles (24 km) N of Norwich
The National Trust

ON the anniversary of her execution, a coach and horses carrying Anne Boleyn's headless ghost is said to rattle through the park of Blickling Hall. On her wooden statue, placed next to that of her daughter Elizabeth on the great staircase, two centuries after her death, is carved the unequivocal claim *Hic nata*. Whatever the truth about the ghostly coach, the claim that she was born here is easily disproved for her family seat was at Hever in Kent. Her father did own the old manor house, built about 1390, which preceded the present building and that is probably the basis of the legend; it seems all the odder considering that the coach was not invented until a century after her death. What is historically certain is that Blickling was the first house to come to the

Thomas Ivory almost entirely rebuilt the Great Hall in 1767, adapting and extending the staircase to match. The figures of Anne Boleyn and her daughter Queen Elizabeth neither of whom had any real connection with Blickling, are nevertheless prominent on the staircase walls.

National Trust under the Country House scheme. Lord Lothian, its last owner and a staunch supporter of the Scheme left it to the Trust when he died in 1940. No members of the family live there now, and the former estate offices serve as the National Trust's headquarters for East Anglia.

Connoisseurs of country houses will immediately spot the affinity between Hatfield and Blickling: Blickling's architect, Robert Lyminge, also worked at Hatfield. Sir Henry Hobart, James I's Lord Chief Justice, bought the old manor at Blickling in 1616 and three years later commissioned Lyminge to build a new house. Lyminge was doubtless influenced by the success of Robert Cecil's great house, but there could not be a greater difference between the settings of Hatfield and Blickling. At Hatfield, the visitor has to work his way round to the main front, gaining the impression of that splendid façade only cumulatively whereas at Blickling the whole façade comes suddenly and dramatically into view. Unlike most of its peers, Blickling is not buried deep in its estate; the winding road from the little market town of Aylsham passes through a wood and then alongside a great sweep of lawn, bordered by two immense yew hedges, that runs up to the house. At night, the effect is particularly striking for the National Trust floodlights the front and the whole looks like a stage setting, framed by the darkness of the nearby woods.

The yew hedges are considerably older than the house itself and so, too, is the dry moat in front, now a delightful sunken flower garden. The moat probably guarded the first manor house on the site, built by Sir Nicholas Dagworth, who bought the manor from Sir John Fastolf, the Norfolk magnate who was later to be immortalized as Falstaff. The dimensions of the old house influenced the shape of the new. Lyminge, for instance, did not adopt the then fashionable E or H shape, as was done at Hatfield, but created instead the relatively old-fashioned internal courtyards. The entrance hall was subsequently rebuilt by the local architect Thomas Ivory. It was Ivory who created a worthy setting for Blickling's famous feature, the great oak

The most spectacular room in a remarkable house, the Long Gallery became a library in the 18th century.

staircase with its guardian figures. Originally, the stairs ascended round the walls of a small well; Ivory boldly cantilevered the entire structure out from the walls so that it seems almost weightless.

The other great feature of Blickling is its superb Jacobean ceilings, in particular that in the Long Gallery. The creator of this remarkable work – some 123 feet in length and divided into thirty-one major panels – has only recently been identified as Edward Stanyan. His bill, dated 10 December 1620, showed that he was paid £38 6s for 'the architrave freese and cornish round about the gallery' and £50 16s for the 'freat seeling'. The Long Gallery also contains the Library which, while it cannot rival that of Holkham, contains an impressive range of treasures, including incunabula amongst its 12,000 volumes. The bookcases and the curious painted frieze are the work of the nineteenth-century artist John Hungerford Pollen. An associate of the Pre-Raphaelites, he was fascinated by Celtic art but much of the elaborate symbolism of his ornamental frieze defies interpretation.

Edward Stanyan's elaborate Jacobean ceiling.

The proportions of the 17th-century house were determined by the original

14th-century building. The affinity with Hatfield is evident in this garden front.

PETWORTH HOUSE, WEST SUSSEX

In the centre of Petworth, 5½ miles (8.8 km) E of Midhurst (A272/A283)
The National Trust

PETWORTH, like Hatfield, is unusual in its proximity to a town. One could almost describe the town as a development of the house, they are so close together. Writing in 1823 William Cobbett, the professional John Bull who had no particular love for the gentry, nevertheless admired Petworth while commenting on its size. 'Lord Egremont's house is close to the town and with its outbuildings, walls and other erections is perhaps nearly as big as the town, though the town is not a small one.'

There has been a house on this site since the early fourteenth century, but the present building is largely the creation of that extraordinary and unloveable man Charles Seymour, sixth Duke of Somerset. Nicknamed the Proud Duke, legend has it that on his journey from London to Petworth outriders went ahead to clear peasants from his path so that their glances would not defile him. He expected to be served on bended knee and even his children were supposed to stand up when speaking to him. The house came to him by marriage – or, to be exact, the money with which to build it. Petworth was part of the vast estates of the Duke of Northumberland and in 1670 the only claimant to this wealth was a three-year-old child, Elizabeth. The unfortunate girl was married off three times before she was sixteen, her third marriage in 1682 being to Somerset. As soon as she came of age, he laid hands on her fortune to build this jewel of a house.

It is typical of the man that he built for show. The back of the house is a hodgepodge of sizes, shapes and periods, traces of the original manor house that

The west front of the house, seen from the park. The town lies behind and actually adjacent to the house.

After the fire of 1714, Louis Laguerre was commissioned to decorate a new staircase in his grandiose style.

The Marble Hall, the only major architectural feature of the 17th-century interior to survive both the fire and the later 19th-century alterations.

had grown over the centuries and which Somerset now left as good enough for domestic offices. The undercroft of the Great Hall also survives, as does the chapel. But the grandiose west front is all his, as is the Marble Hall. It lacks Clandon's icy grandeur and the friendly beauty of Houghton, but is still a masterpiece and is the only major internal feature of Somerset's day to survive a disastrous fire in 1714 and the restless alterations of the mid-nineteenth century.

For Somerset's work only provided a platform for his successors. A century later, the third Earl created the Carved Room. Here are now displayed Grinling Gibbons' superb limewood carvings, emphasizing in particular the portraits of the Proud Duke and his wife. In creating the frames for the pictures, Gibbons virtually created sculpture, so deep is his carving, all but detaching his distinctive

Petworth is particularly rich in Grinling Gibbons' work.

fruit and flowers from their background. Horace Walpole, no casual bestower of compliments, thought that this room displayed 'the most superb monument of his skill'. Next to the Carved Room is a shrine to perhaps England's greatest painter, J.M.W. Turner. His friend and patron, the third Earl, gave him a room as a studio and he came to love Petworth, visiting it again and again in the 1830s, leaving among much else that marvellous evocation of sunlit calm, *The Drawing Room at Petworth*.

'Capability' Brown, designer of Petworth's landscape.

In 1751, three years after the Proud Duke's death, Capability Brown was commissioned to lay out the gardens. Out of many designs, one was chosen in 1752 and in successive contracts over the next five years the gradual development of this enormous project can be traced. Brown's goal of a 'natural landscape' was achieved so successfully that it took in even William Cobbett. Visiting this entirely artificial development seventy years after it was completed, Cobbett, practical farmer and connoisseur of landscapes though he was, described the park as 'very fine ... consists of a parcel of hills and dells which Nature formed when she was in one of her most sportive moods'. It would have amused and delighted Capability Brown to have been mistaken for Mother Nature.

KNOLE, KENT

At Tonbridge end of Sevenoaks, just E of A225,
25 miles (40.2 km) from London
The National Trust

DID Mervyn Peake ever visit Knole, one wonders? For this vast, rambling house seems the ideal model for that phantasmagoric castle Gormenghast, with its endless Earls of Groan, which is central to his trilogy. Certainly the house provided the background for one of the odder pieces of English literature, Virginia Woolf's *Orlando*, the story of the immortal boy/girl who changes sex through the centuries, symbolic of a family's transmission of identity. Virginia Woolf gave the manuscript to her friend Vita Sackville-West, and it now lies in a place of honour in the house. Vita Sackville-West herself left a lively portrait of the house in *Knole and the Sackvilles* which conveys the spirit of a great house as experienced by one who was born in it.

The core of Knole was built sometime in the late fifteenth century by Thomas Bourchier, Archbishop of Canterbury. Queen Elizabeth I gave the house to her cousin, Thomas Sackville, later Earl of Dorset. Sackville has some literary merit as the author of *Gorbuduc*, reputedly the first tragedy in English (and probably the least read); but he made his money as a politician under Elizabeth and James I, pouring his wealth into extending and decorating Knole.

Apart from its great size, what is most striking

*The size of the house is vast, its variegated roofscape resembling that of a village
or small town.*

Built between 1605 and 1608, the staircase was a decided novelty for its day.

about the house is its interior gloom. This is partly the result of its architecture, but it is also the deliberate policy of the National Trust. Although the family of the present Lord Sackville continues to live in the house, maintaining the four-century link, Knole passed into the possession of the Trust in 1946. It was faced with the problem of conserving one of the richest and rarest collections of historic fabrics in Europe. As Lords Chamberlain to the monarch, the Sackvilles had a valuable perquisite – the right to discarded royal furniture – in particular the rich hangings and upholsteries. To protect these priceless fabrics, some now in their third century, light is reduced to a minimum. Attendants are armed with torches to illuminate details for visitors with a more than casual interest – an altogether odd experience, but one which was shared by others in the past. Horace Walpole, that indefatigable visitor of country houses said of Knole 'I worship all its faded splendour, and enjoy its preservation'.

One of the striking illustrations of this 'faded splendour' is the great staircase. It was an innovation in its time. People were accustomed to stairways that disappeared upwards from view and this splendidly balustraded creation, seemingly

The Green Court. The gatehouse is known as Bourchier's Tower, after Thomas Bourchier who began building Knole.

hanging in space and visible over all its length, must have been startling. This effect was increased still further by the *trompe l'oeil* decorations on the walls enclosing the staircase. Today the whole has faded, decorations on walls and on three-dimensional elements alike, and in the underwater gloom the eye is deceived for a moment into accepting the entire structure as a painted decoration.

The Cartoon Gallery, with its six copies of Raphael's cartoons, probably from the studio of Daniel Mytens.

CHATSWORTH, DERBYSHIRE

½ mile (0.8 km) E of village of Edensor off A623,
4 miles (6.4 km) E of Bakewell,
10 miles (16 km) W of Chesterfield

THIS enormous house achieved its final form in an almost absent-minded fashion. The original Elizabethan manor (built by Bess of Hardwick and her husband William Cavendish, about 1552) remained largely unchanged until 1686. This was the house which Mary, Queen of Scots, would have known, for it formed one of her many prisons. The restored Mary's Bower is a relic of this period.

Then, in 1686, the fourth Earl – created Duke of Devonshire for his support of William of Orange – began to pull down the south front. It would seem that, initially, he intended to do little more than put up a fashionable façade. But as many a rich man before him had found, the temptation to put his own impress on his day through the medium of bricks and mortar proved overwhelming. Gradually, one front after another was demolished and built in the current style, the whole operation being finished just before his death in 1707. It was a curious process. The actual ground plan remained unchanged and it was as though the building was shedding one skin to grow another. The exquisite model of the house now on display in the north entrance hall illustrates what is not obvious in the house itself. The ad hoc approach to building resulted in a grave miscalculation with the east front some nine feet longer than the west. This would have resulted in a curiously slanting front had not the architect resolved the dilemma by building a bow to hide the fact.

The next great stage of building was that undertaken by the Bachelor Duke – William, sixth Duke of Devonshire (1790–1858). The wealth of the Cavendishes, already vast, was augmented by skil-

The west front, probably designed by Thomas Archer, with the personal aid of the 1st Duke.

94

The State Drawing Room. The ceiling is by Laguerre and the tapestries, based on Raphael's cartoons, were woven at Mortlake.

ful marriages, and drawing on this fortune the Bachelor Duke initiated a programme which was to last nineteen years. Among much else, he brought into being the enormous north wing, very nearly as big as the original house. Particularly valuable from the historian's point of view is the record he made of his work, in the form of a series of letters to his sister. In a relaxed, fluent, amiable manner he takes the visitor round from room to room, pointing out not only what was already there, but the changes he had made. He had some salty things to say about the grandiloquent work of some of his predecessors. The Duke's handbook remained unpublished for nearly 150 years until the present Duchess incorporated large sections of it in her own account of the house. Between these two records, both informal but well informed, the reader obtains an unusual insight into the running of, and the alterations made in a great house over a climacteric period.

Chatsworth thus has two essentially different parts: the stiffly formal seventeenth-century building and the still grand, but more humane nineteenth-century wing. The State Rooms lie on the upper floor. Regarding this range of vast rooms, the Bachelor Duke was sorely tempted. 'The State Dining Room was never dined in that I know of – the first room of this great unappropriated apartment which consumes in useless display the best habitable part of the house. What bedrooms might have been made here, with the South sun and beautiful views! I was much tempted – but finished conservatively by repairing the sinking floors and threatened ceilings.'

Displayed in these rooms is the whole function of a great house as an instrument of prestige. The eye is at first dazzled by the sheer wealth and detail of decoration – the gold leaf and stamped leather, the rich tapestries which cover the walls. But looking beyond and behind them is to see that these vast rooms are simply empty cubes with little or no clues as to how they were used socially. How, where and when did their occupants conduct their more intimate affairs – eating, dressing, washing – when not engaged in public display?

The incredible wealth of treasures at Chatsworth produces a kind of numbness (the house takes two hours for the visitor to see). One takes away a kaleidoscope of rich impressions. The extraordinary Oak Room, a whim on the part of the Bachelor Duke, who bought the carved oak panel-

William Spencer Cavendish, 6th Duke of Devonshire (1790–1858).

ling of a German monastery on impulse, and then built a room around them for which successive owners have rather desperately tried to find a use. The superb Chapel, built between 1688 and 1693 and totally unchanged. The chilly splendour of the sculpture gallery, filled mostly with nineteenth-century examples. The incredible Library, superlative in appearance and superlative in its collection. The nineteenth-century Dining Room with its curious ceiling which, the Bachelor Duke observed, gives the room the appearance of a cabin trunk's interior, and the modern sculptures and paintings, including Lucien Freud's disturbing 'Large Interior w.9'. However, two images remain: a small, cheap photograph of a smiling young woman holding a cockerel and, beside it, the large portrait of a handsome young man in uniform. The young man was the Marquess of Hartington, heir to the house, but killed in action in 1944. The woman is his wife, born Kathleen Kennedy, sister of the man who later became President of the USA, and who was herself killed in an accident in 1948, leaving as a record only this hasty snapshot, now placed among the portraits of the 500-year line of Cavendishes.

Louis Laguerre painted the upper part of this splendid hall, with scenes from the life of Julius Caesar, from 1692, since when it has not been changed. The ceiling was discovered to be sagging in 1936 and required two years work to make it safe.

WOBURN ABBEY, BEDFORDSHIRE

In Woburn; 8½ miles (13.6 km) NW of Dunstable on A50,
42 miles (67.5 km) from London off M1, exit 12

THE Marquess of Bath was undoubtedly the first owner of a great house to try and make it pay for itself. But equally undoubtedly John, thirteenth Duke of Bedford, was the first to carry the idea to its logical conclusion and turn his house into an entertainment industry. In consequence, Woburn Abbey is again and again cited in horror by purists as the fate worse than extinction awaiting great English houses. One wonders whether the more vociferous critics have ever visited the place. On approaching the house from the village of Woburn there is no evidence whatsoever of the notorious fairground or its ancillaries. Humphrey Repton did his work well nearly 200 years ago, the gently undulating hills and carefully sited copses masking a wide range of tourist activities which would have astonished him.

The reception area of the house is low key. A much thumbed copy of the Department of Employment's *Hours and Conditions of Work* hangs beneath stern portraits of the Russell family, but there is little else to show that one has entered an organization which employs 250 people, spends at least £1 million a year in maintenance and has to cater for about a million visitors each year. Behind that velvet front is a very steely business. The house, with its fantastically rich collections, is only one of many attractions. There is a complete gallery of antique shops, as well as craft shops, a restaurant and a zoo – each contributing its portion to the

The grotto – a delightful fantasy, built 1619–41 and possibly designed by Inigo Jones, then working for the 4th Earl.

The 4th Duke commissioned these views of Venice by Canaletto, which have hung in the room designed for them since 1800.

upkeep of this massive, grey, Palladian mansion.

Woburn Abbey, as its name indicates, was part of the great monastic plunder of the sixteenth century. It stands on the site of a Cistercian monastery; the abbot was incautious enough to make an uncomplimentary remark about Anne Boleyn and after his execution, the abbey and lands were given to John, first Earl of Bedford. Already well supplied with fat estates in the West Country, Bedford did nothing with his gift; nor did his descendants until, in the early seventeenth century, the fourth Earl moved from London to avoid the plague. Woburn was convenient for the capital, and successive members of the Russell family engaged in the English aristocrat's traditional pastime of tearing down and rebuilding. The main front of the house as it appears today is largely the work of Henry Flitcroft, who was commissioned in 1747 to transform the old monastic buildings into a modern residence. Following the shape of the Cistercian cloister, the house was built around a quadrangle – a shape it retained until 1950 when the entire eastern range was demolished because of dry rot.

The Russell family has always been at, or near, the centre of political activity, sometimes profitably – as in the case of the first Earl – and sometimes decidedly unprofitably. William, Lord Russell, for instance, died on the scaffold 'a martyr to the Romish fury'. It has also bred its share of eccentrics like the twelfth Duke, who pulled down nearly half the house and who lived like a viceroy 'isolated from the outside world by a mass of sycophants, servants and an eleven-mile wall'. With his accidental death in 1953 it seemed as though Woburn had come to the end of its life as a family home, for the Russells now incurred death duties of £5 million. It was to pay off that enormous debt that the thirteenth, and present Duke of Bedford in effect founded the stately home industry.

In his minority the Duke had suffered decidedly from the Russell eccentricity. He describes in his autobiography how he was well into his teens before

Queen Victoria's dressing room, named after her visit to Woburn. Today it contains Dutch and Flemish paintings.

he even saw Woburn, much less realized he was a possible heir. He was working abroad successfully as a fruit farmer when he learned he had succeeded to both the title and the estate. Apart from the incredible tax due, the house itself was in an appalling condition with priceless art treasures jumbled with piles of junk in dusty rooms. Running the place as a home seemed to be out of the question. 'Although there would be a substantial income available to the family, there seemed to be no way of devizing any arrangement which would permit the furbishing and upkeep of Woburn, which to me was the only object worth preserving in the whole estate.'

There was, in fact, one possible way of doing so, but it had to be done wholeheartedly. 'I paid a couple of incognito visits to houses open to the public. However, they were all doing it on the theory that the sooner the visitors were in, the sooner they would be gone, the quicker you got the money and goodbye. That was not the way I intended to do it. I wanted to make people enjoy themselves, give them service and value for money and make sure they would come back again. If this enabled me to live in my ancestral home, everyone would be satisfied.'

In the event, everyone *was* satisfied: the public, who found a fascinating new venue; the taxman, who eventually collected his £5 million and the

Originally built by Holland as a conservatory, this sculpture gallery was created by the 6th Duke.

The little Chinese dairy, built by Henry Holland during extensive rebuilding of the house in 1787.

Russells, who again had a family home – even though they share it with a million or so people every year. In 1974, the Duke retired and his son, the Marquess of Tavistock, inherited the great building together with its problems.

The Marquess is a businessman – a stockbroker – who runs Woburn, too, as a business. His office, once the ballroom of the Abbey, is now its administrative nerve centre combining comfort, efficiency and historic interest in equal degree. (In it are two enormous desks pushed back to back, for the Marchioness takes a prominent part in the running of the machine.) He emphasizes his acceptance of, and his pride in the remarkable tactics used by his father to save his ancestral home. Public opening is essential to the survival of the building. And anyway, as he has said 'What could I do with fourteen sitting rooms, half a dozen galleries and the rest? It was different in the past. They used to have endless country house parties, with people moving in flocks from one to the other. Today, most of us are working.'

The English art of compromise has resulted in the salvation of Woburn.

THE EIGHTEENTH CENTURY

SEATON DELAVAL, NORTHUMBERLAND

$\frac{1}{2}$ mile (0.8 km) from the coast at Seaton Sluice,
between Blyth and Whitley Bay (A190)

THERE can scarcely be a more prosaic piece of real estate than the flat lands a few miles north of Newcastle. Tynemouth to the south, and Blyth to the north, extend industrial pincer movements towards the cold North Sea. But between the arms of these pincers, scarcely a mile from the coast, lies Sir John Vanbrugh's great house. It has a quality of eeriness due partly, no doubt, to the fact that for nearly 150 years this house – the seat of the 'gay Delavals' – was empty save for the ghostly memories of past revels. An immense fire gutted the interior in 1822 and it remained boarded up and shuttered until 1950 when its owner, Lord Hastings, partially restored it.

But it also has a quality of fantasy which arises from the nature of the building itself. Here, one

In front of one of the wings, partly facing the other, with the vast courtyard stretching away to the right.

The sense of a stage setting is carried strongly into the great hall, still marked by the fire of 1822.

The south front portico, less sombre than the overwhelming ceremonial approach of the north front.

feels, as at Blenheim, Vanbrugh was as much playwright as architect, in his mind's eye seeing some titanic stage set. Admiral George Delaval invited him north, after buying the estate from a cousin in 1717, to design a house 'for the entertainment of our old age' and, despite its great size, this element of entertainment seems to dominate all else. To get the full flavour one should approach the great north front on foot. The vast wings on each side of the equally vast court rise slowly to encompass the walker, until the steps leading up to the main entrance are reached. One feels a bar or two of *Parsifal* should be played as one enters the hall. Splendid as it must have been at the height of its

glory, today it has an additional poignancy for the stone walls and statues are still marked by that great fire over a century and a half ago.

Admiral Delaval never saw his house completed for he died in a fall from his horse in 1723. The house in due course passed to a collateral branch of the family whose descendant, the twenty-second Lord Hastings, initiated the massive work of restoration, with the help of grants from the Historic Buildings Councils. The family established itself in the west wing where, Lord Hastings records: 'My son was born in 1960, the first time Delaval Hall had known such an event since my ancestress Rhoda Delaval gave birth to a son in the West Wing in 1757!'

HOLKHAM HALL, NORFOLK

2 miles (3.2 km) w of Wells,
s of Wells-Hunstanton road (A149)

A wartime aerial photograph, taken about 1943, tells the story of Holkham Hall in starkly dramatic terms. Immediately below lies the ordered mass of the great building, beyond it a dark belt of trees, a lighter belt of sand-dunes, and then the sea. The trees protect house and estate from the almost ceaseless north wind that roars in off the North Sea, while the house itself is in almost arrogant control of its environment, classical perfection set down among the bleak salt marshes. Indeed, at the time it was being built, a contemporary described the estate as 'a desert where two rabbits fight for one blade of grass'. Yet in due course this 'desert' became the laboratory for one of the most influential of all agricultural experiments, that initiated by 'Coke of Norfolk' in the early nineteenth century.

Thomas Coke, later Earl of Leicester, conceived the idea of the house while on the Grand Tour in Italy in 1713. He met William Kent and they determined to transport Rome to England, to build the perfect Palladian house in Norfolk, but it was not until 1734 that the foundations were actually laid. Coke died in 1759 before the interior was completed, but his imprint is firmly upon the house.

Holkham is a cerebral building, with every tiny detail planned for overall effect. The result from the outside, particularly viewed from the north, is cold and somewhat repellent. For the locally made bricks that were used have weathered little over the years and what might very well appear as a warm yellow-brown under a brilliant Italian sky seems stark and sombre under the steely light of East Anglia.

The impact is all the greater when one enters the

The south front with its fountain tableau, and the formal gardens, created by Nessfield in the 1850s.

The Marble Hall, understandably Holkham's most famous feature, with its fluted columns of Derbyshire alabaster.

State Rooms. The superb Marble Hall is a triumph. Kent used the rich alabaster of Derbyshire, in hues of ivory, purple and green for his material and drew upon the temple of Fortuna Virilis for his inspiration. This is no pastiche or copy, but rather a subtle transmutation of ideas. An 1830s guidebook remarked 'When the Person who shews this house is engaged, the company is conducted into the Vestibule. The curious visitor will not regret the time while contemplating the various subjects in the room.' The twentieth-century visitor will be as well rewarded.

Financially, Holkham has suffered less than many of its peers, largely because of the extraordinary richness of its library. The collection of books was originally made by the first Earl of Leicester on his Italian tour. From time to time, it allowed the Cokes to pay off a hungry Chancellor like so much Danegeld. Almost every sale made headlines in the national, and sometimes the international press. The most outstanding was the recent sale of the Leonardo da Vinci codex, which realized £2.2 million, to pay off death duties. An American bought this manuscript outbidding representatives from both Florence and Milan, but the British Museum was able to purchase the fourteenth-century Holkham Picture Bible so this, at least, remains in England. But the library is still one of the richest in the country. In 1947 the current Earl introduced was was then a revolutionary new idea, that of selling slides of the library's treasures in what the librarian, W.O. Hassall, somewhat fulsomely described as 'a miracle of cultural democracy'.

Thomas Coke, the agriculturalist, was a son of the

The north dining room is in the form of a cube, with a central apse for the serving table.

The saloon, the principal State Room, with its original wall covering of Genoa velvet.

builder and succeeded on his father's death. The Great Barn, designed for him in 1790 by Samuel Wyatt, is still a main feature of the grounds. It was here that Coke entertained his neighbours during the annual sheep shearings, when they discussed those new agricultural techniques that quietly revolutionized European farming. There was, in fact, a sheep shearing here in 1978. Appropriately enough, the estate has made a special collection of farming implements for the interest of visitors. And continuing that very Norfolk vein of practicality is the Holkham Pottery. Started by Elizabeth, Countess of Leicester, in 1957, it is now a flourishing industry, employing many local people.

HOUGHTON HALL, NORFOLK

13 miles (20.9 km) E of King's Lynn,
10 miles (16 km) W of Fakenham (A148)

THE position of Houghton Hall near the coast of Norfolk perfectly illustrates that concept of the 'country house' as an essentially urban structure in rural surroundings that typifies the eighteenth century. Coming through the forbidding pine forests around Sandringham, one arrives at a little cluster of white-painted estate houses grouped before an elegant wrought iron gate, the whole resembling something from one of the Grimm fairy tales. The approach to the house lies down a narrow lane, and there, rearing up from a great stretch of lawn is a building that would not look out of place in Paris. The paradox continues: the house is set in extensive parkland but the oaks, though formally planted, seem to melt into their agricultural background.

For such a perfectly designed, symmetric house, it is odd to find that it is the work of three architects. Colen Campbell was the main figure, but Thomas Ripley and perhaps James Gibbs had a hand in it between 1722 and 1735. But behind them all lay the forceful, unifying mind of England's first prime minister, Robert Walpole. His portrait by John Wootton hangs in the Stone Hall. Wootton has placed him in a rural setting (despite the incongruity of lavish gold braid on his coat) conveying the impression that Walpole wanted to make – that of a

Houghton – an outstanding example of Palladian architecture – is an urban house in a rural setting, for it is surrounded by its working Norfolk agricultural estate.

The Marble Parlour, with chairs of Genoa silk velvet and Chinese armorial plates; Rysbrack carved the overmantel.

bluff, no-nonsense Norfolk squire. But behind that heavy, rather complacent face was a shrewd mind and a highly cultured spirit. Improbably enough, the core of the great art collection of the Hermitage in Leningrad was assembled here among the Norfolk turnips by Walpole himself. His grandson, the third Earl of Orford, was eccentric to the point of insanity and, running the estate deep into debt, sold off the collection to Catherine the Great. Her portrait, too, hangs in the house – a miniscule return for such a great loss.

The Green Velvet Bedchamber is the work of William Kent, who designed the bed and painted the ceiling. The tapestries are from the Brussels workshop.

This was the only major depredation of the contents, and the house and furnishings today continue to reflect a subtle blend of solidity and elegance, itself an expression of Robert Walpole. Unlike his neighbour Coke at Holkham, he had no use for the brick that is the indigenous building material of Norfolk. It was good enough for the core of a wall but for its shell he wanted stone and obtained it from Yorkshire. Fortunately, Houghton was only a few miles from the bustling little port of King's Lynn: the hundreds of tons of Aislaby sandstone required were cheaply floated down from Whitby and carried by expensive oxcart only over the last short lap.

The interior of the house is all of a piece, for William Kent was not only responsible for the decorations, but made most of the furniture and the marble fireplaces. The stuccoist, Artari, was brought in to carve the moulding of the Stone Hall (see frontispiece), and the sculptor, Michael Rysbrack, created the fireplace. Both men worked on the similar Marble Hall at Clandon, but that great chamber is cold and uninviting, compared to Houghton's Stone Hall. This certainly does not lack majesty, but partly through its proportions, and partly through use of the warm Yorkshire sandstone, one feels this is a room that can be lived in as well as looked at.

The house has been open to the public only since 1976 and, like other owners, the Marquess of Cholmondeley has sought to create some additional attraction for the public. Here, the choice has been not lions or giraffes or other exotica but the shire-horses which created the agricultural wealth of Norfolk. Joe Green, who started as a stableboy at Houghton in 1926, returned in 1972 as head groom with the heartfelt remark 'It's like coming back to life again.' The great, gentle creatures browsing in the paddocks give their own air of solidity, of the permanent relationship between house and land.

The Great Staircase is in mahogany, one of the first uses of the wood in England. The murals are the work of Kent.

BURTON CONSTABLE, HUMBERSIDE

In Burton Constable, $1\frac{1}{2}$ miles (2.4 km) N of Sproatley,
$7\frac{1}{2}$ miles (12 km) NE of Hull (A165)

IT is singularly appropriate that among the ghosts reputedly thronging Burton Constable (including an entire Roman legion clanking its way through the woods by the drive) should be that of William Constable, a benign presence in the Gold Bedroom. For the interior of the house as it now appears is very largely his work. Born in 1721, William Constable was possessed of a lively, enquiring mind – a type which, coupled with great wealth, did so much to advance the cause of science in the eighteenth century. He was a fellow of the Royal Society, for which he was proposed by no less a person than Banks, its formidable president. He was a member of the Lunar Society, a friend and patron of Joseph Priestley and a correspondent of Jean-Jacques Rousseau. In the Museum Rooms (originally a theatre) are displayed some of the objects which reflect his manifold interests – the interests of an aristocratic, scientific dilettante which, in due course, would provide a stimulus for the Industrial Revolution and all that came afterwards. There is the travelling medicine chest which he used on his long foreign trips, from which he brought back yet more ideas for the embellishment of his home. In the Muniment Room are displayed drawings by the craftsmen he employed in the massive programme of modernization that he embarked upon – sketches and plans by Robert Adam, James Wyatt, Capability Brown and Thomas Chippendale. All are of intrinsic interest, but even that is increased by the fact they are related to the building around them. One can enter the Drawing Room on the west front and see there the chairs Chippendale designed. Similarly, one can turn from Capability Brown's sketches and see in the gardens the actual lakes and bridges that he planned.

It is not known for certain when, or by whom, this massive house was built. It was probably the work of Sir Henry Constable, who died in 1606. His portrait in the Great Hall shows the house in the background, giving substance to this theory. But he was almost certainly building on, or near, a much older house. The Constables acquired the manor of Burton in the early twelfth century, and the oldest

The Long Gallery, built by Cuthbert Constable in 1736; the frieze is derived from the Bodleian Library, Oxford.

In contrast with much of the interior, the exterior remains an early 17th-century building.

It was William Constable (b. 1721) who transformed the interior of the Stuart house of his ancestors into 18th-century elegance, exemplified by the Yellow Drawing Room

surviving part of the existing house, Stephen's Tower, dates from this period. Externally, however, the house is one of the many portentous, red brick buildings which reflected the power and wealth of newly rich Elizabethan magnates.

William Constable, either through a fine feeling for history, or a preference for expending energy in decoration rather than construction, left all this untouched. His father, Cuthbert, began the work of change by creating the Long Gallery, as late as 1740 (and curiously old-fashioned he must have seemed to his contemporaries in doing so). William took up the task in the 1750s, which continued for the next twenty years. The last of his work was the Great Ballroom, which Wyatt built between 1775 and 1776, the plasterwork for which was carried out by an Italian, Giuseppe Cortese. Chippendale designed the furniture specifically for this room, charging £1,000 for it. So proud was William Constable of his newly furbished home that, in 1778 when Chippendale finished his work, he had notices printed saying that the house would be open to the public.

CONSTABLE BURTON, NORTH YORKSHIRE

On A684 between Leyburn and Bedale on A1

ARCHITECTURALLY, Constable Burton has had a decidedly odd history. Although the Wyvills have been established here for centuries, the building is purely Georgian, supposedly the result of a mistake. In 1762 Sir Marmaduke Wyvill commissioned John Carr to make certain alterations to the existing Elizabethan manor, agreed a sum of £1,500 for the work, and sensibly went away while it was being done. In his absence, however, Carr demolished almost the entire building, a single room surviving to greet the owner on his return. Wyvill seems to have been a remarkably tolerant man for Carr, instead of being driven off with contumely, was actually commissioned to build an entirely new house – at a cost of £10,000. Presumably, this was his original intention but in any event he did well by his client, creating this faultlessly Palladian villa.

But if Constable Burton is an almost textbook example of the eighteenth-century classical revival (so much so, that its elegant bridge and loggia might have come from the hand of Palladio himself) the means whereby it was brought back to life in the 1970s is itself a classic illustration of the problems facing the owners of country houses, and the solutions available. As with so many of its peers, the house was rented out between the two World Wars. On the death of the tenant, the Wyvills decided to take up residence and restore the house. Although the garden had been well cared for, the house had been less well maintained. 'For six months we lived in the Oak Room [its panelling was all that survived from the Elizabethan mansion]. No heating. No water. Nothing!' Over the following years, room after room was brought back into habitable condition. Furniture was unearthed after having been stored for more than forty years. In the interim, the boom in antique prices had given much of it very considerable value. 'But it belonged to the house – that was the whole point of the operation.' Restored, it now completes the whole.

The house, as a listed building, was eligible for a grant for repairs but, in return, had to be open to the

Constable Burton, showing John Carr's perfect Palladian front. The double stair leads over a bridge to the loggia.

The Drawing Room, with its distinctive chimney piece and plaster ceiling in Adam style.

public for the statutory minimum of thirty days a year. Unlike great houses of the order of Blenheim or Woburn, where visitors can be channelled through the State Rooms away from private quarters, smaller houses have literally to be open throughout. But the owners feel it is a fair return.

Although some 400 people visited Constable Burton in 1981, their combined entrance fee is only a drop in the ocean. How, then, is the place funded? The estate consists of 3,000 acres so the traditional industry of farming underpins the whole. The letting of shooting rights and accommodation also contributes greatly to the upkeep of the house. Between August and January the house is full; but it also entails a great deal of unglamorous hard work, the Wyvills necessarily adding the skills of hoteliers

to that of traditional hosts. These funds are channelled into the house, evident from its superb condition. It would be an interesting actuarial exercise to calculate what it would cost the State to keep it in equivalent condition.

The gardens are a major attraction – currently, there are eighty-two varieties of daffodil alone – and are frequently visited by horticultural enthusiasts. The neglected vegetable garden has been brought back to life. Labour costs today make it uneconomical – it is almost certainly cheaper to buy vegetables in the superb local markets than to pay for labour to grow them. But, like the antique furniture that has been given new life in an old setting, the restored vegetable garden is part of the whole vision of Constable Burton.

BLENHEIM PALACE, OXFORDSHIRE

sw end of Woodstock which lies 8 miles (12.8 km)
n of Oxford (A34)

THERE are two main approaches to Blenheim Palace from the beautiful little town of Woodstock, the Hensington Gate and the Triumphal Gate. The first-time visitor should unhesitatingly take the Triumphal Gate entrance. The high street leads into a stone quadrangle surrounded by a high wall. There is no indication whatsoever of the stupendous vista which instantly opens up as the visitor passes through the gate. In one swift glance one is aware of Capability Brown's landscaped park, green slopes running down to a great lake, a bridge and in the distance the spires, triumphal arches and swagger-

This is the ceremonial fulcrum of the palace for, standing with one's back to the great portico, one looks across the Grand Bridge towards the Column of Victory. Capability Brown, with a certain insensitivity, grassed over the forecourt, but the 9th Duke repaved it between 1900 and 1910. The finest talents of the day were used at Blenheim.

ing turrets of what seems to be a township. The vista resolves itself into a carefully planned theatrical setting, touched with fantasy, the perfect framework for the biggest drama of all, Vanbrugh's Blenheim Palace.

This, the only non-royal, non-episcopal palace among the hundreds of great houses in England, also challenges two basic English predilections: their dislike of monumental buildings and their suspicion of military heroes. A statue, perhaps, or a plaque is usually considered more than adequate. It is doubtful if many of the thousands who visit Blenheim each year are aware of its significance. For this great Baroque palace is a token of the nation's sense of pride and relief after the victory of Blenheim in 1704, sufficient to make it forget its normal thriftiness.

Built at royal Woodstock, it was the gift of Queen Anne to her triumphant general, the first Duke of Marlborough. No contract was drawn up – it scarcely seemed necessary, for were not the Queen and Sarah, Duchess of Marlborough, the best of friends, confiding in each other as Mrs Morley and Mrs Freeman? But the friends fell out, and bitter arguments later developed as to who owed whom for what, and a second battle of Blenheim ensued, which David Green has brilliantly chronicled in his history of the house.

Vanbrugh lost this battle. He also had his differences with the Duchess, and her continual criticism of his work brought the matter to a head. The finest talents of the day were employed in the embellishment of Blenheim – masons, and carvers such as Grinling Gibbons – but funds were curtailed and work remained unfinished. Vanbrugh resigned in a rage in 1716, and Hawksmoor was left to complete it. When the Duke died, Sarah was left with a vast sum of money and power 'to spoil Blenheim in her own way' as Vanbrugh put it bitterly. She was involved in lawsuits with over 400 people connected with the building of Blenheim, and by the end of her life had spent £300,000 on the palace, three times Vanbrugh's estimate. But she finished this enormous building, the most splendid relic of its age.

The State Dining Room. The ceiling and murals were painted by Louis Laguerre; some of the figures peering over the balustrades are imaginary, others are caricatures and others, again, portraits – among them Laguerre's own, much as Verrio included himself in the Heaven Room at Burghley.

Vanbrugh's massive Baroque palace, built to commemorate Marlborough's victory in 1704.

This aerial view of Blenheim captures the stupendous scale of the concept.

GORHAMBURY HOUSE, HERTFORDSHIRE

2¾ miles (4.4 km) w of St Albans, off A414

THE visitor to Gorhambury sees a relatively modern house, actually built in 1777 but seemingly new for it has recently been refaced in sparkling Portland stone. But behind that calm front is a tide of English history and great names: Ethelred the Unready; Verulamium; Bacon and Skakespeare; Elizabeth I and Henry VIII. The original manor belonged to King Ethelred who gave it to the Abbot of St Albans. The name derives from Geoffrey de Gorham who built the first known house about 1130, doubtless using materials from the nearby Roman ruins of Verulamium. After the dissolution, it was bought by Sir Nicholas Bacon, father of the great writer, who promptly built a more splendid house higher up the hill. Elizabeth visited him there, and twitted him about its small size, where-

The formal façade of Gorhambury has changed little since Robert Taylor completed it in 1784.

Most of the paintings in the Yellow Drawing Room are contemporary with the house, and include Joshua Reynolds' group portrait of the four children of James, 2nd Viscount Grimston.

The Library, with its white marble mantelpiece by Piranesi. The books were catalogued on Francis Bacon's system.

upon he expanded it in time for her next visit. The cost of the royal reception is recorded in the accounts as £577 6s 7¼d for barely four days.

In due course the old manor house came to Francis Bacon. When not conducting affairs of state (he was Lord Chancellor under James I) writing his *Essays* and, according to his devoted band of disciples, penning the plays of Shakespeare, Bacon devoted much time to the house. He had no children, and when he died the house was bought in 1652 by the improbably named Sir Harbottle Grimston, a successful lawyer. The family flourished, and in 1777 the third Viscount Grimston followed the fashion of his class and day and built the present Palladian house. The old Tudor home was abandoned, though its ruins remain and its history pervades the later house. Here is the earliest-known, documented portrait of an Englishman, that of Edward Grimston, dated 1446. Gorhambury also contains an extensive collection of family portraits, running from the fifteenth to the twentieth century, together with enamelled glass windows from the old mansion and mementos of Francis Bacon.

He lives on in the Library which is catalogued according to his epochal divisions of knowledge, and it was here that seven of Shakespeare's plays were discovered. The oldest in private possession, they are now on permanent loan to the Bodleian Library, Oxford, but photographic copies are kept in the house to maintain the link between Francis Bacon (Lord Verulam) and the enigmatic playwright from Stratford-on-Avon.

Ruins of the original 16th-century manor, built by Sir Nicholas Bacon and preserved in the park.

SUTTON PARK, NORTH YORKSHIRE

8 miles (12.8 km) N of York,
4 miles (6.4 km) from Easingwold on B1363

HANGING in the entrance hall of this trim, early Georgian house is the engraving of a building with a tantalizingly familiar appearance and name – Buckingham House. The central block is, in fact, the precursor of Buckingham Palace and a previous owner of this house, the late Major Sheffield, was the descendant of that Duke of Buckingham whose London home was to become the monarch's palace. The Sheffield seat was at Normanby Park in Lincolnshire but the size of that house, together with the ravages created by open-cast mining in the park, caused the purchase of this house when it came on the market in 1963. The family had originated large properties in Lincolnshire and in Yorkshire, so the move was historically satisfying.

Sutton Park is built on the edge of the little village of Sutton-on-the-Forest – as neat as the house itself and built of the same clamp-fired, rose-coloured bricks. Probably built by Thomas Atkinson in 1720 on the site of an Elizabethan mansion, it was

The Tea Room with its collection of Imari porcelain.

This exotic domed structure is, in fact, an ice-box, double-shelled and mostly underground for coolness.

Sutton Park's garden front. This modest, yet impressive, early Georgian classical brick mansion was built on the site of an Elizabethan manor in the 1720s, to which two elegant wings were added in the mid-18th century.

extended by two graceful wings in 1760 but has since remained unchanged. All the furnishings were brought from Normanby Park, including the elegant bookcases designed by Smirke especially for that house, and the series of family portraits, both maintaining continuity and giving the house an unexpected weight. The rooms have an easy eclecticism: the splendid Chinese Room (with rare wallpaper dated about 1760) boasts an Adam fireplace, also from Normanby Park, and the Dining Room has been completely recreated.

The gardens come as a complete surprise. The casual eye would assume they were contemporary with the house, but they have been designed entirely since 1963. The first year was spent uprooting neglected evergreens, reducing the number of gravel paths, taking in a large piece of the park which included a fine cedar tree – this gave the new garden an instantly mature look. An outstanding discovery was the splendid brick ice-house, one of the finest of its kind still in existence. Now restored, this circular pit, eighteen feet deep with a double-domed brick roof, despite its prosaic function, conveys a deeply mysterious atmosphere. Had its domestic use been unknown, one wonders to what religious purpose it would have been assigned.

CLANDON PARK, SURREY

At West Clandon 3 miles (4.8 km) E of Guildford on A247
The National Trust

IF Blickling was the first country house to come to the National Trust under the Country House Scheme, Clandon was the object of the Trust's first great restoration project when, over a period of two years, some £200,000 was spent. That sum has long been surpassed at Erdigg but Clandon established the precedent.

The Earls of Onslow bought the land in 1542 and erected a handsome manor house upon it. In the eighteenth century an Onslow married a wealthy heiress and promptly invested her money by building, about 1730, a house more in keeping with the times. It was a massive, square, red brick building designed by the Venetian Giacomo Leoni, in grounds laid out by the ubiquitous Capability Brown. The third Earl abandoned the place in the nineteenth century and for over forty years it went to ruin, its gardens overgrown and chimneys blocked solid by birds' nests. When the fourth Earl succeeded to the title in 1870, he recorded 'I was the first person who for many years was allowed to enter the house. It was almost bare of furniture and all blinds and curtains had perished.' The house temporarily returned to its former splendid life at the end of the Edwardian era, but was again virtually abandoned during the 1930s. Immediately after World War II the sixth Earl and his wife made a courageous attempt to bring Clandon back to life: one of the showpieces of the house are the dyed US army blankets out of which Lady Onslow made curtains for the huge windows. But the attempt was hopeless and in 1956 the house was given to the National Trust.

The immense work of restoration was put in hand. Between 1927 and 1945 much of the interior decoration had disappeared under a thick coat of whitewash, beneath which lay even more layers of paint smothering the original. John Fowler, the interior decorator who was entrusted with this delicate work, remarked: 'In a house of this age it is usual to discover in the State Rooms five or six layers of paint, and in the more domestic parts as many as twenty or thirty.' A major feature of Clandon is the remarkable Marble Hall where

Leoni's austere façade, to which was added the clumsy porch and porte cochère in the 19th century.

The original colours of the saloon ceiling – blue, pink and yellow – survived the ubiquitous whitewash.

plasterwork by the Italian stuccoists, Artari and Bagutti, had been worked to imitate marble. Under the whitewash that liberally covered this, Fowler discovered that two distinct kinds of plaster had been used – 'icing sugar' for the ceiling, and a rougher plaster for the walls – allowing a subtle distinction that had been eliminated by the whitewash brush. The 'coldest house in England' lived up to its reputation when cold water used for cleaning off the whitewash froze in sheets to the walls.

There have been at least a dozen changes in fashion since the house was first decorated, and it was decided to choose the early eighteenth century as the period to which the body of decoration should be related. The house is probably unique in that the much of the colour scheme for this time is known, and the work was faithfully and skilfully carried out by local craftsmen, repeating what their predecessors had executed two centuries before.

The subtle, intangible but vital link with the family is still maintained. The present Earl and his family live in the old Home Farm, itself an Elizabethan farmhouse only a few hundred yards from the house, and on the site of the original manor.

Clandon's splendid Marble Hall, patiently restored.

THE NINETEENTH CENTURY

ARUNDEL CASTLE, WEST SUSSEX

In Arundel, 9 miles (14.5 km) w of Worthing,
10 miles (16 km) e of Chichester

THE perils and prizes of high office could not be better illustrated than by the brilliant, bloody, turbulent history of the Fitzalan Howards, lords of Arundel Castle. Three of them were beheaded; one was probably poisoned (he was canonized in 1970 as St Philip Howard); two nieces, Anne Boleyn and Catherine Howard, finished up on the block, and their unscrupulous uncle Thomas, the third Duke, would have followed them had not death taken off his ferocious master, Henry VIII, the day before his own execution was scheduled.

And through all this, the family kept its hold on the building which was begun by Roger de Montgomery about 1067. It was probably Montgomery who built the castle's most distinctive feature, the motte and bailey, and from a distance Arundel Castle looks like a child's vision of what a castle should be like, with the Duke's standard flying

The Library. Ecclesiastical motifs are strong : even the chimney pieces resemble chantries.

Arundel Castle stands dramatically on its chalk spur above the river Arun.

proudly from the bailey when he is in residence. In the latter part of the eighteenth century, however, and throughout the nineteenth, the entire interior underwent a remarkable transformation. In 1777, plans were made to restore the half-ruined building into a worthy ducal seat. Successive dukes, sharing the Victorian belief that they knew far more about medieval buildings than people who lived in the Middle Ages, turned Arundel Castle into the romantic Victorian idea of a medieval castle.

Henry, the fifteenth Duke, brought the vast programme to a conclusion in 1910, and not content with 'restoring' the castle, he built the enormous

Catholic churches in Arundel and Norwich, capital of his titular county. For, by one of the engaging ironies of English history, the premier English duke who traditionally arranges the great state ceremonies for the sovereign – who, by law, must be Protestant – is a Roman Catholic. Everywhere in the castle is evidence of this long compact with the Old Faith, and deep preoccupation with religion. The great library resembles the interior of a Gothic church – even its fireplaces are in the form of Perpendicular chantries – and one of its exhibits is a portable altar. The library contains one of the richest collections of books on Catholicism in

England. In the so-called Victoria Room there is a portrait of Cardinal Newman by Millais. The eleventh Duke rebelled against the prevailing religiosity and turned the private chapel into a splendid but unwelcoming dining room about 1795. The fifteenth Duke restored the status quo by building a new private chapel in what has been described as the most perfect expression of the nineteenth-century Catholic revival. The third Duke, who sent Catherine Howard to her death, peers out sourly from among the group of family portraits in the Picture Gallery while in the East Drawing Room are the mementos of Mary, Queen of Scots – a prayer book and gold rosary which she bequeathed at her execution to her fellow Catholics.

It is in the Fitzalan Chapel in the parish church, however, that the paradox of a Catholic duke in a hostile Protestant country is brought home. Built in 1380 (and desecrated in 1643) it can only be entered from the castle and, with the tombs of its dukes from the fifteenth to the twentieth centuries, is quite different in atmosphere from the body of the church.

The much restored Norman keep and barbican.

The Private Chapel: its stained glass, by John Hardman Powell, is inspired by that of Canterbury Cathedral.

Illuminated prayerbook and rosary carried by Mary, Queen of Scots, at her execution and bequeathed to the Howards.

CLIVEDEN HOUSE, BUCKINGHAMSHIRE

3 miles (4.8 km) from Maidenhead,
2 miles (3.2 km) N of Taplow on B476
The National Trust

CLIVEDEN House has entered political mythology as one of the great centres of manipulation – of 'fixing it' – between the two World Wars. Whether or not the so-called 'Cliveden Set' really did alter the course of affairs in the 1930s or whether, in Byron's words, its members 'thought they were running the world because they went to bed late', is still a matter of debate. But this great house, on its terrace high above the Thames, really was a magnet for the powerful as well as the merely fashionable, the gifted as well as the idle. Churchill, Henry James, Balfour and Rudyard Kipling were among those who joined the house parties presided over by the remarkable Nancy, Lady Astor.

The two previous houses on this site were both almost totally destroyed by fire. George Villiers, second Duke of Buckingham, built the first house, creating the vast terrace which his successors were to utilize. A baroque character –

A man so various that he seemed to be
Not one but all mankind's epitome

he killed the man he was cuckolding while the man's wife calmly looked on. (The shape of a duel sword, cut in the turf near the house, commemorates the event though the duel took place miles away near Putney.) His house was destroyed in 1795 and its successor in 1849. The present house was built by Sir Charles Barry (co-architect of the Houses of Parliament) in 1850 and was bought by the

The south front, overlooking the immense parterre and the river beyond, with the Borghese balustrade. Sir Charles Barry built this beautiful Renaissance house in 1850 for the Duke of Sutherland.

The Gothic Drawing Room, originally designed by Sir Charles Barry.

American millionaire, William Waldorf Astor, in 1893.

Although American by birth Astor, his son, and in particular his son's wife Nancy, became more English than the English – so much so that Nancy Astor became the first woman to enter the House of Commons as an MP. Astor senior spent vast sums improving the work of his predecessor, and remained true to the tycoon's creed that money really could buy anything. He cast his eye on the balustrade of the Villa Borghese in Rome and bought it for his splendid new house. The Italian government took the Borghese family to court for alienating a national work of art and received the Solomonic judgement that while the statues on the balcony were 'important antiques' the balcony itself was simply a 'decorative object'. Visitors to Cliveden may therefore lean on stonework which may once have been leaned on by Pauline Bonaparte.

Nothing prepares the visitor for the stupendous view from Cliveden's terrace. Entering from the Taplow Road, one is immediately confronted by a statuary group that almost achieves the level of kitsch – the vast Fountain of Love, created by an American sculptor living in Rome, depicting young maidens, in various stages of undress, reeling from the effects of Love. Astor commissioned this group specifically, which does raise doubts as to his aesthetic taste.

Beyond the fountain, the house becomes visible, compact and solid; and beyond that is the upper terrace with its startling view over the Thames which drew a gasp of admiration from John Evelyn, that connoisseur of vistas. It reminded him of

Thomas Story's Fountain of Love.

The stunning view overlooking the river Thames.

Frascati. The huge parterre, or formal garden, below does indeed seem designed for confidential political murmurings. It would be quite impossible to eavesdrop on those acres of lawn. The surrounding gardens are all heavily wooded – though carefully framing and not obscuring the vista – and from the opposite bank of the Thames the whole looks natural. But as with so much of the English landscape, what seems natural is of most careful construction. A visitor to Cliveden in 1793 described how the newly-planted trees were all anchored by ropes 'otherwise the Winds would tear 'em down'.

Astor's preference for classical antiquities are evident throughout the garden: Roman sarcophagi lined up dramatically against a dark yew hedge; the great Queen Anne's vase; the exquisite little Blenheim Pavilion and Octagon Temple. The interior of the house reflects the pastiche of the garden. Visitors to Cliveden may perhaps be startled by what appear to be copies of the Blenheim tapestries, commissioned by the Duke of Marlborough to commemorate the War of the Spanish Succession. Other, very similar tapestries were also to be found at Stowe and Stanmer, as well as a number of German schlosses. The canny Brussels weavers turned out a number of these tapestries, altering details to suit the buyers – and selling them to both sides.

Lord Astor left the house to the National Trust in 1942, and the Trust leased it in 1966 to Stanford University, California, honouring the Astors' wishes that Cliveden should be used 'to bring about a better understanding between the English-speaking peoples'.

ALNWICK CASTLE, NORTHUMBERLAND

In Alnwick, 30 miles (48.3 km) N of Newcastle, off A1

LOOMING up from the buttercup-strewn meadows along the river Alne, the exterior of Alnwick Castle is all that a medieval castle should be. There are even alert watchmen on the battlements, eighteenth-century copies of much earlier figures. But the interior is the Victorian idea of an Italian Renaissance palace. This contrast is the work of the fourth Duke of Northumberland. Like so many of his fellow aristocrats, he embarked on the Grand Tour of Italy in the early nineteenth century, and was much taken by the distinction between the exterior of most Italian palaces with their stark, uncompromising strength, and their luxurious interiors. He determined to create the same effect in Northumberland; it cost him more than a quarter of a million pounds in the 1850s, but he succeeded.

There has been a castle at this vital spot at least since the time of the Norman Conquest. In the early fourteenth century the Percy family, father and son, built most of the exterior which now stands. The first major changes took place during the eighteenth century when the first Duke of Northumberland transformed it from a castle into a residence. Canaletto's painting of the castle, now hanging in the Music Room, shows it shortly before these alterations. The greatest change is in the land itself, for the crags and crevices between castle and river, so evident in Canaletto's painting, have since been smoothed out by the busy Capability Brown, advancing the cause of civilization into the Northumberland wilds.

The great barbican or main gateway is unchanged, an entrance so important that it is virtually a little castle in its own right. Looking down through the gaps between the timber baulks of the bridge which it guards, one can see part of the recently excavated moat far below: once, it would have connected with the river. Through the less dramatic

The castle viewed across the river Alne. The bridge to the town, protected by the castle, lies to the right.

The utilitarian Guard Chamber transformed into a Renaissance interior. The pavement is of Venetian mosaic.

carriageway to the right, the visitor emerges from the shadow of the walls to see a great expanse of turf – the outer bailey – and rearing up from it the keep and the main mass of the castle. It is here that the Renaissance begins. The entrance hall of the keep is modest enough but it leads to the splendid Grand Staircase, each of whose treads is a single block of stone, twelve feet in length, from the nearby Rothbury quarries. The walls are lined with coloured Italian marble, and Venetian mosaic covers the floor of the Guard Chamber into which the staircase

The barbican, built about 1440, in effect a small independent fortress with its own garrison astride a moat.

The Grand Staircase, begun in 1861.

leads. Carved, gilded ceilings replaced Adam's designs. Time has a disconcerting habit of revealing truth in architecture as in everything else. To the fond eye of the fourth Duke and his Italian advisers, Staircase and Guard Chamber would have seemed perfect Renaissance structures but to the modern eye they are unmistakably nineteenth century, beautiful though they may be. The two great statues of Britannia and Justice in the Guard Chamber could be the product only of Victorian England.

There is an ordered richness throughout, cul-minating in the superb Red Drawing Room. The casual visitor will simply accept that order as though it were organic: the architect's drawings tell another story. The ceiling of the Drawing Room is composed of polygonal panels, but the room itself is irregularly shaped, having been altered to fit the design of the ceiling – a Procrustean solution that sums up the confidence and wealth of architect and patron.

The vast castle is no museum. Not only is it a family residence but it is also the heart of a huge working estate, including 6,000 acres of woodland and 160 farms. Tucked onto it, almost as an extension of it, is the little town of Alnwick. A large proportion of the local people earn their living, in one way or another, directly from the castle, and living here is rather like living in a garrison town where everyone is aware of the status of everyone else. The Percy lion, with its extraordinary tail sticking out like a poker, still guards the bridge that used to be the only access to the town from the north – the access that takes the traveller immediately under the walls of the barbican and its watchful statues.

MUNCASTER CASTLE, CUMBRIA

1 mile (1.6 km) SE of Ravenglass village on A595

THE name of Muncaster gives us a clue to its origin, for 'caster' is an indication of the Roman fort that once existed here, on the height which simultaneously defends the entrance to the Esk valley, and the little port of Ravenglass below. Today, Ravenglass is a quiet place, but as the Roman town of Glannoventa it was a vital link with the sea road that lapped Britain's coast.

Approaching Muncaster from the south is like driving over the edge of the world. It is necessary to go further and further south, before being able to turn north around the great mass of Furness Fells. Even today, the most direct route is from west to east along the Esk valley, and there is small wonder that the Romans took care to police this approach. (There are the ruins of another solid castle at Hardknott pass, about half way along the valley.) The remains of the fort are probably buried deep below the present castle, for coins of around AD 300 have been found.

The locations of military sites give a spectacular bonus: it was important to see the enemy at a distance and to have a clear expanse for retaliation. Muncaster enjoys such a bonus, and the views from the terrace can only be described as breathtaking. Edward VII, who prided himself on being widely travelled, proclaimed this the best view in Europe, and Ruskin impulsively described it as the 'gateway to Paradise'.

The castle went through a familiar cycle of change. The first post-Roman fort would have been built about 1260 by the Pennington family, to whom the lands had been granted half a century earlier. The massive pele tower – still a conspicuous feature of the garden front – was part of the considerable enlargement undertaken in 1325. During the Wars of the Roses Sir John Pennington gave shelter to Henry VI. According to legend, the King was wandering lost after the battle of Towton and was brought to the castle by a shepherd. Among the treasures shown at Muncaster is a fragile glass dish of indisputable age, known as the Luck of Mun-

The garden front of the house, as redesigned by Anthony Salvin, in pink granite.

The octagonal library, built in 1780 on the site of the medieval kitchen, with some alterations by Salvin in 1862.

The famous view from the terrace which led Ruskin to describe Muncaster as 'the gateway to Paradise'.

caster, supposedly given by the monarch to Sir John. It raises many questions. Why did the King express his thanks in so inexpensive a manner? How did the legend arise that the family's luck would hold good only as long as the bowl is intact?

Apart from the pele tower, little remains visually of the original building. Muncaster began its transformation into a purely residential building in the eighteenth century and then, in the nineteenth century, was 'medievalized' by Anthony Salvin. His patron, the young fourth Earl of Muncaster, Gamel Pennington, gave Salvin a very wide brief but died in 1862, at the early age of thirty-one, before the work was carried out. The Trustees of the estate, less enamoured with Gothick and shocked at the proposed expense, trimmed down Salvin's design to the benefit of the old building. Built in pink granite, Muncaster is still very much Salvin's work but without the flamboyance of Alnwick, remaining firmly within the vernacular tradition.

The Trustees' restraint, or Salvin's innate good sense, saved the beautiful octagonal library, built about 1780 on the site of the medieval kitchen. Salvin made a few interior alterations, but contented himself mostly with disguising the external shape. Much of the house's contents reflect the taste of an individual connoisseur, Sir John Ramsden, the sixth Baronet, who built up the collection between the two World Wars. But the drawing room, built on the site of a courtyard in 1861, contains one of the most complete collections of a family's portraits in England. Among them is one of the unfortunate Protector, first Duke of Somerset, father of Jane Seymour and thus grandfather of the short-lived Edward VI. The fifth Baronet married a descendant of Somerset – hence his portrait here.

HUGHENDON MANOR, BUCKINGHAMSHIRE

1½ miles (2.4 km) N of High Wycombe
The National Trust

ONE of the problems for houses in the care of the National Trust is that, although they are well maintained and their future assured, inevitably they become museums as the families drift away. This is by no means the case at Hughenden Manor for although no member of the family lives there, it is pervaded throughout with the spirit of Benjamin Disraeli who bought it in 1848, spent his happy marriage here, and also died here in 1881.

Dizzy loved the place with a deep, personal, abiding love. But its acquisition was something of a contradiction in his nature. This Italian Jew with the affected manner, the ringlets and the dandified clothing, made his mark on the ultra-conservative British, not by playing down his mannerisms but by exaggerating them. The acquisition of that quintessentially English institution, the 'country house', was doubtless initially a political gesture, the means whereby he showed the Commons, as he moved towards the leadership of the Tory party, that he too had his stake in the country. But, once established in it, his home ranked second in affection only to his beloved wife.

The house is pleasant and interesting, rather than distinguished, and were it not for that vibrant presence, it probably would not rank high on the

Francis Grant's portrait of Disraeli, 1852.

tourist circuit. It began life as a farm house, a 'house in the country', and was converted into a 'country house' (a distinction very real to the British) in 1738. John Norris, the antiquary, then acquired it, favouring the fashionable Gothick style beloved by the Disraelis.

The house cost Disraeli £35,000, most of it obtained on loan. Politics kept him in London, and much of the work of modernizing the house and laying out the garden fell on his wife, Mary Anne Disraeli. But husband and wife thought as one in all such things, and the garden is a perfect expression of them both. Sadly, Mrs Disraeli did not live to see the moment of the house's greatest splendour, and the almost unprecedented honour done to her husband when Queen Victoria visited the house in 1877. It was an informal affair – as much as Victoria's visits ever were informal – and she graciously planted a tree in her favourite's beautiful garden.

There are no great works of art at Hughendon,

Hughendon Manor – the entrance front. Disraeli's nephew, Coninsby, made some later alterations to the house.

The Library: in Disraeli's day this was the drawing room.

but the house is filled with mementos which throw a sudden, intimate light on some large historical canvas. In the so-called Berlin Congress Room is the cherry-wood fan, signed by all the statesmen who attended the Congress. Disraeli called the hall his Gallery of Friendship, for along it are hung portraits of the friends and allies he made through a long and active life. There are two portraits of Lord George Bentinck – that great 'swell', sportsman, politician and dandy – who generously came forward at the necessary moment and lent Disraeli a large sum to help buy the house.

Room uses have been switched around since Disraeli's time: what was the drawing room, with its distinctive Gothick arches, is now the library and vice versa. But Disraeli's study, which he called his workshop, is exactly as he left it. Victoria made a return visit to the house after his death, almost, one feels, as a pilgrimage and spent a long time in this comfortable but modest room. One of the pictures displayed is that famous cartoon in *Punch* that is a key to the relationship between these two so very different people. In 1876 Disraeli secured for her the title of Empress of India and Tenniel's witty cartoon, *New Crowns for Old*, shows Disraeli as an exotic Oriental pedlar proffering the splendid crown of India to his queen.

Disraeli called his study 'my workshop'.

BELVOIR CASTLE, LEICESTERSHIRE

7 miles (11.3 km) WSW of Grantham between A607
(to Melton Mowbray) and A52 (to Nottingham)

ITS superb site, high on a dramatic ridge above the Vale of Belvoir gives this castle its name. William the Conqueror granted the land to his gallant standard bearer Robert de Todeni, who built the first castle, and whose massive stone coffin still resides here. But the castle itself has dizzily changed its form at least four times. The original Norman motte and bailey evolved into a crenellated fort, and in this form it came into the Manners family (later Earls and Dukes of Rutland) by marriage. Totally slighted after the Civil War it had been rebuilt by 1668, only to be demolished in the late eighteenth century as part of a massive rebuilding programme. Work began again in 1801, to Wyatt's design, and was all but completed when a great fire broke out on the morning of 16 October 1816. By the time it was brought under control, it had destroyed the entire north-east and north-west fronts, the great staircase and – far worse from an art history point of view – a number of great paintings, including Titians and Van Dykes.

The architects for much of the present building could best be described as talented amateurs, for they were a clergyman, the Reverend Sir John

Belvoir (pronounced 'beaver'), a magnificent martial building with many neo-Gothic features, is the romantic 19th-century concept of a medieval castle.

This aerial view of Belvoir castle shows its dominant position overlooking the Vale. This wooded hill-top has been a stronghold since the Norman conquest, for the first castle on this site was built by William the Conqueror's standard bearer.

Thoroton, and the Duchess of Rutland herself. Between them, this unlikely pair created a Gothic fantasy. The castle looks best either from a distance, when its multiple turrets do indeed seem lifted from a medieval illumination, or seen from inside. The details within are superb, from the Guardroom at the entrance, with its sweeping arches and stairways, to the richly worked Elizabethan Saloon, which started a new fashion for Louis XIV taste. Some

The Elizabeth Saloon, named after the 5th Duchess.

The Grand Staircase, with its portraits of the 5th Duke, and his wife Elizabeth, who played an important role in the creation of this Regency castle.

The Elizabeth Saloon: detail of the painted ceiling.

idea of the loss of paintings in that fire can be gained by the quality of the collection which survives, including works by Holbein, Teniers and Gainsborough. Altogether it is a curious coincidence that this castle, the ultimate in mannered reconstruction, should belong to the same family that owns Haddon Hall, an untouched survivor from the Middle Ages.

MELDON PARK, NORTHUMBERLAND

6½ miles (9.6 km) w of Morpeth off B6343

ON 17 October 1832, a flint glass box containing a newly minted sovereign of the reign of William IV was sunk in the turf of a plateau above the little Wansbeck river in Northumberland. Above this box, a massive two-ton block of honey-coloured stone was carefully lowered and the home of Isaac Cookson was begun.

The architect, John Dobson, would undoubtedly have been nearby. He had walked the grounds for an entire month, scrambling down the steep slope to the river and up again many times, looking for the perfect site. The fifty-year-old cedar tree planted then flourishes still, presenting something of a chronological problem to those unaware of the early nineteenth-century skill in horticulture. Dobson was then in his forty-fifth year and with a solid reputation behind him. He had done for his native Newcastle what Nash had done for London, creating a series of elegant streets whose design, though classical, was within the idiom of their day. After designing Meldon Park he built Newcastle Railway Station, establishing the archetypal railway station whose influence was to be felt around the world. On this October day, however, he was initiating the kind of work for which he now tends to be better known – building a home for a gentleman of substance.

Surely there can be no other period like the nineteenth century for an efflorescence of architectural styles. One tends to associate the entire century with the Gothick flamboyance which characterizes

Meldon Park, with Dobson's Ionic entrance porch.

its later stage. But here, in Northumberland, four years before the young Princess Victoria came to the throne, Dobson created for his patron a restrained, elegant, classical building – a perfect example of the Greek Revival.

Meldon Park is deceptively simple, a square building whose only external decorations are the severe Ionic columns of the porch. But this simplicity is the result of immense care. None of the features which disfigure houses from this date onwards – drainpipes, sewage pipes and the like – are visible: all are carefully tucked away behind that mellow stone. Even the gutterings are hidden by an elegant balustrade.

Inside, the house has the same indifference to its rural environment as Houghton. This is not so much a country house as a house in the country. The great rooms overlooking the secluded valley are not simply urban but metropolitan in feeling. The doors of the library are carefully disguised by false book-ends, a device which tends to disconcert bibliophiles. But Meldon Park is very much a home, a fact to be put squarely to Dobson's account. In the words of the owner (a descendant of the Isaac Cookson for whom it was built), 'The house is easy to live in and very domestic: there is no oppression caused by grand scale for although the rooms are spacious they remain private, intimate.' The great vegetable gardens are slowly being brought back to life, one of its features being an enormous hollow wall which could be heated. As at Constable Burton, it forms a traditional part of a living country house.

The Library; the double doors are disguised as bookcases.

EASTNOR CASTLE, HEREFORD & WORCESTER

5 miles (8 km) from M50 (exit 2),
2 miles (3.2 km) E of Ledbury
on Hereford–Tewkesbury road (A438)

IT seems scarcely possible that the classical façade of the British Museum in London and the Gothic extravaganza of Eastnor could have come from the same hand. But the architect in both cases was Robert Smirke. The British Museum façade more closely approximates to the original inspiration than does Eastnor: no one could possibly mistake this for anything but the nineteenth-century whim of a rich man. But it is consistent throughout, even though its most characteristic feature, the great Gothic drawing room by Pugin, was not added until more than thirty years after Smirke had finished.

The work was commissioned by Lord Somers, who recorded in his detailed notebook on 23 June 1812, 'I laid this day the first ashlar ornamental stone, and placed under it a piece of money of Queen Elizabeth, my family having settled in Eastnor about that reign.' He provided some meticulous and interesting figures regarding its construction: 20,000 tons of stone and mortar were used in the first eighteen months, and 250 men were employed constantly over six years at a cost of £750 a week. The stone was brought from quarries in the Forest of Dean by barge and then ox-wagon at an overall

Pugin decorated the Drawing Room in 1849, drawing even more heavily on the 'Gothic' image than had Smirke.

The equestrian armour is Italian, about 1640. The mural decoration may be derived from a Saracen banner.

The massive structure of the great towers as seen from the south front.

cost of £12,000. Shortage of timber, much of it swallowed up by the Napoleonic war, forced Smirke to improvize. He used cast iron stanchions for the roof trusses, their first known use in this manner, and they are still in good condition.

Eastnor is particularly interesting for its collection of art and armour. The third Earl Somers was an Italophile and brought back, among other treasures, tapestries from the Gonzaga palace in Mantua (originally woven for Catherine de' Medici) and a superb suit of armour belonging to the Visconti family of Milan.

Eastnor is also a refuge for the works of a Victorian painter who, immensely successful in his day, is undeservedly all but forgotten now. G.F. Watts was a friend of the third Countess and painted a number of frescoes for the Somers' London house at Carlton Terrace. The existence of five of these was reported to the Crown Commissioners in 1927 and in 1938 Joachim von Ribbentrop, the German ambassador then occupying the house as part of the German embassy, reported four more that had been boarded over. The frescoes were taken down in 1966 when the house was being drastically altered, and in 1976 were placed, on loan, in the Staircase Hall at Eastnor. Apart from the major collection now housed in the artist's home at Compton in Surrey, they form the biggest collection of the paintings of a man once known as 'England's Michelangelo'.

Eastnor, built in 1812 by Robert Smirke – the medieval castle as seen by a 19th-century romantic.

THE TWENTIETH CENTURY

CASTLE DROGO, DEVON

4 miles (3.2 km) NE of Chagford, 6 miles (1.6 km) S of A30
The National Trust

JULIUS Charles Drew, builder of Castle Drogo, was undoubtedly a nicer character than Sir William Thynne, builder of Longleat. But separated though they are by blood, time and customs, they nevertheless bear a curiously strong resemblance to each other. Both were self-made men, doggedly amassing a fortune. And both, having made that fortune,

The vast entrance with the motto Drogo Nomen Et Virtus Arma Dedit *(Drewe is the name and valour gave it arms).*

proceeded to spend a substantial part of it in creating a vast house. They also have another affinity, for one marks the beginning of a process and the other the end. Thynne's house was the first of the prodigy houses; Drew's house – one may fairly confidently predict – is likely to be the last castle built not only in England but in Europe.

Julius Drew, born in 1856, was very much a child of his time for he made his money out of the rapidly expanding British empire. Like so many young men of his day he 'went out East', to China, on behalf of his uncle Francis Peek in order to learn the mysteries of tea buying. Returning to England, he decided to set up business on his own. The result was the Home and Colonial Stores, its history exactly coinciding with the swift apogee and decline of the empire (it has now been absorbed into a well-known chain of stores). By the age of thirty-three Drew was so rich that he could retire and devote himself to his heart's desire. He had made his millions at about the same time, and in the same market, as Sainsbury and Lipton. Sainsbury stuck to business; Lipton threw his money into the sea in pursuit of yachting prizes, but Drew turned his money into stone.

His motives were common among self-made men from the time of classical Athens onward: having made his pile he wanted to backtrack and create, retrospectively, a dignity for it. This was the period when the would-be aristocrat did not simply buy land but also sought a title that would give a mellowness to his new-found wealth. Genealogists made a good living from that desire: a delighted Julius Drew was told that he was descended from the Drewes of Drewsteignton in Devon. They were descended, in their turn, from a certain Drogo or Dru who had 'come over with the Conqueror'.

The castle seen from below : the river Teigh lies behind and below, where the ground falls steeply away.

Given the ramifications of genealogy in a small, crowded and ancient island, there is no particular reason why the story should not be true. Julius Drew consulted a lawyer and, by deed poll, added that vital final 'e' to his name that made him of Norman descent. And as Julius Drewe of Drewsteignton he embarked upon the most ambitious of projects, the building of a castle to go with the name.

The construction of fake castles had become an obsession among the landed gentry during the nineteenth century. In 1857, Sir George Gilbert Scott had inveighed against what he called 'the monstrous practice of castle-building, unhappily not yet extinct. . . . The largest and most carefully and learnedly executed Gothic mansion of the present day is not a sham fortress such as those of twenty years back, but it is a real and carefully constructed medieval fortress capable of standing a siege from an Edwardian army. Now this is the very height of masquerading.' Born just one year before Scott made his protest, Drewe would have grown to manhood at a time when 'the castle' most perfectly expressed the pretensions of power. And being essentially a conventional man, when he came to

Lutyens designed all the details at Castle Drogo, even the furniture in the kitchen.

build his own house, he too thought in terms of something 'capable of standing a siege from an Edwardian army'. Nothing would be sham about it; from its granite foundations upward, everything must be real, everything must work as in a medieval fortress – even the portcullis over the main entrance to the castle.

He found the ideal architect in Edwin Lutyens. Behind him Lutyens already had some solidly successful commissions, while ahead of him lay the viceregal splendours of Delhi. It is a curious coincidence that this great architect should have built the last of the English castles and the last architectural expression of imperial power. Drewe and Lutyens admired each other, shared the same romantic but practical nature, had the same objective – and fought vigorously throughout the building of Castle Drogo, the tension between them proving creative, not destructive. As Lutyens said in one of his outbursts, 'I am very keen about your castle and must "fight" you when I know I am right.' The two of them made dozens of sketches through which it is possible to see the dream gradually becoming reality. At one stage Lutyens suggested cavity walls; Drewe insisted on authenticity throughout, even where it could not be seen. The walls were accordingly of solid granite with a necessary reduction in overall size.

The site was of pre-eminent importance: even in the twentieth century, a castle had to *look* as though capable of withstanding a siege. Drewe found it in the form of a great bluff above the gorge of the river Teigh. Even today the land that falls away from the castle is still wild – heather and pine-clad – with the stark moors rising on the other side of the gorge.

Work began in 1912. No one could have guessed that western civilization was plunging towards irrevocable change. But neither the cataclysm of World War I, nor the dizzily fragmenting society of the 1920s could halt the work. Drewe's eldest son was killed on the Western Front in 1917, but there were other heirs to ensure continuity and work went forward until 1930. After twenty years working upon his dream Julius Charles Drewe, descendant of Drogo the Norman, had exactly one year in which to enjoy his creation before he died in 1931. His son inherited it, and in due course his grandson who, while continuing to live there, gave the castle to the National Trust and so ensured the survival of Castle Drogo.

Lutyens' use of granite and oak to give a feeling of clean strength is shown in this corridor. Drewe's portrait hangs at the end of the passage.

Lutyens' genius has created a synthesis, not a pastiche. The overall external effect is undeniably house rather than castle, emphasized by the generous window spaces (simultaneously reminiscent of Hardwick Hall and Coventry Cathedral). But the internal details are those of a castle that has been modified to the comforts of twentieth-century life. Throughout, granite and wood are the media that speak of the past. There is a clean sparseness about the rooms which, flooded as they are with light, is curiously exhilarating. Lutyens panelled two rooms, the drawing room and the dining room, to soften the omnipresent granite. His genius extended to the smallest details: in the kitchen he designed not only the beautiful solid beech table, but also the pastry boards upon it – and even the draining boards by the sink. He placed the large portrait of Drewe on the landing of the splendid stairway so that the visitor ascends to it as to a shrine or memorial. But while this is Lutyens' design, it is Drewe's dream made substantial, one man working through the mind of another as always has been the case with the building of a great house.

ACKNOWLEDGMENTS

The author and publishers would like to thank the owners or tenants of these houses for permission to include them in this book.

Photographs were supplied and are reproduced by kind permission of the following institutions, museums and photographers:

Aerofilms 116–7; 139; John Bethell Endpapers (Blenheim Palace), 16 above, 17, 18–19, 65, 93 below, 128 below, 130, 136 below, 137 above, 145; Janet and Colin Bord 66 below left, 67; Neil Burton 58; Country Life 46 above; Christopher Dalton 26 left, 78, 123 below, 127; English Life Publications Ltd 21, 28, 29, 61, 131, 132 left; Fotobank/English Tourist Board 15, 30 (Trevor Wood), 52 (Jon Wyand); Hever Castle 68, 69 below; Michael Holford 62; Angelo Hornak Copyright page (Sarah, Duchess of Marlborough), 72–3, 109 left (by kind permission of the Marchioness of Cholmondeley); Jarrolds 14, 22, 23, 79, 98, 99, 104; A.F. Kersting Frontispiece (Stone Hall, Houghton Hall), 24 left, 25, 30 below, 33 below, 39, 40, 47, 53, 56, 57, 69 above, 76, 77, 81, 85 above, 88, 94, 95, 97, 100, 103, 106 left, 107, 108, 109 right, 122, 126 above and left, 132 right, 138, 140; Loseley House 60; Sally and Oliver Mathews 125, 143 above right, 144; National Motor Museum, Beaulieu 31, 32, 33; National Portrait Gallery 90 right; National Trust 34 (John Bethell), 38 above right, 38 below (Olive Kitson), 66 above left, 71 below, 84 (Jeremy Whitaker), 86–7 (Jeremy Whitaker), 92 (Horst Kolo), 93 above (John Bethell), 123 above (Jeremy Whitaker), 128 above, 129 (Angelo Hornak), 136 above (John Bethell), 137 below (John Bethell), 142, 143 left, 146 (Peter Mansfield), 147; Photo Precision Ltd 64 right; Edwin Smith 10, 41, 59, 64 above left, 70, 83 below, 90 above left, 101, 102, 143 below; Transglobe 54; Trustees of the Chatsworth Estate 96; Weidenfeld and Nicolson Archives 12 (Jeremy Whitaker), 24 right, 26 right (Cressida Pemberton Pigott), 27 (Cressida Pemberton Pigott), 30 above, 36, 37 (Kerry Dundas), 38 above left (Kerry Dundas), 42–5 (Cressida Pemberton Pigott), 46 left (Cressida Pemberton Pigott), 48 (Cressida Pemberton Pigott), 49 (Susan Lund), 50, 51 right, 63 (Kerry Dundas), 64 below left (Derrick Whitty), 74–5 (Cressida Pemberton Pigott), 82 (Derrick Whitty), 83 above (Derrick Whitty), 85 below, 90 below left, 91, 105, 106 right (Kerry Dundas), 110–113 (Cressida Pemberton Pigott), 114, 115, 118–119 (John Bethell), 120–1 (Cressida Pemberton Pigott), 124, 126 below right, 133 (Cressida Pemberton Pigott), 134 (Jeremy Whitaker), 135 (Cressida Pemberton Pigott), 141 (Cressida Pemberton Pigott); Jeremy Whitaker 51 left; Whitbread Collection 8 (Bridgeman Art Library); Andy Williams 35, 55, 71 above, 80; David Worth Regional Map 7; Woodmansterne Publications Ltd 16, 66 right

GLOSSARY

aumbry Recess or cupboard in a church wall, originally for keeping sacred vessels, books etc.

bailey The walled area outside a keep but within the curtain wall (q.v.). See also *motte*

banqueting house A small house in a garden, or small room in a house set aside for informal parties

barbican The fortified outwork of a castle

bargeboard Endboard of a gable, usually decorated

Baroque Richly decorated style, originating in Italy *c.* 1600

battlements (also called crenellations). Regular openings in the parapet of a building for purposes of defence. Later (i.e. 18th and 19th centuries) used as decorative feature

belvedere Literally 'beautiful view'. Usually, a small detached building, built to command an attractive view

Brown, Lancelot 'Capability' (1715–83), architect and landscape gardener. His naturalizing style later became formalized

cantilever Projection (as in a staircase) supported at the wall end only

casement Window hinged on one side as opposed to sash

castellation See *battlements*

Chinoiserie Light-hearted imitation of Chinese motifs, usually 18th century

classical Style originating in, or derived from, ancient Greece or Rome

clerestory Windows along the upper part of a hall or church nave

corbel Projecting segment, or supporting block of a beam, usually decorated

crowsteps Stepped, or staggered, end of a gable, common in East Anglia due to its Netherlandish origin but rare elsewhere

cruck Primitive, massive form of timber-framing consisting of matched, curved timbers in an inverted v form

curtain wall Main defence wall entirely surrounding a castle

dissolution Technically, the 'resumption' into Crown hands of monastic properties, beginning with the Act of 1536 and completed by 1540

dais The raised platform at the end of a hall, separating the lord and his family from the household

Domesday book Census made for tax purposes in 1086

feudal system Pyramidical form of land tenure, based on relationship between lord and vassal. See also *manor*

friary House of mendicant, or preaching order, usually in or near urban locality (e.g. Dominicans at Blackfriars)

gable Triangular upper section of wall supporting a sloping roof

garderobe Wardrobe, also containing privy

gatehouse Main entrance, usually to fortified house or monastery

Gothic, Gothick Gothick was the first manifestation of the Gothic Revival, beginning *c.* 1750 and continuing into the early 19th century, relying largely on decoration. The Gothic Revival itself was based on greater archaeological knowledge and recreated medieval Gothic structurally. See also *Salvin, Smirke, Pugin*

Great Hall Main room of early medieval house

ha-ha Sunken fence, or ditch, designed to separate garden from park and so keep cattle out without visual boundary. Invented early 18th century

Kent, William (1684–17) Architect, sculptor, landscape gardener. Originated new style of landscape in England in contrast to formal, geometric gardens

Laguerre, Louis (1663–1721) He and his mentor Verrio (q.v.) covered acres of ceiling and walls with highly-coloured allegories, satirized by Pope. Came to England in 1683

lantern Turret, pierced with windows

Laroon, Marcellus (1679–1772) English-born genre painter

linenfold 16th-century panelling in form of hanging folds of linen

louvre (sometimes *louver*). Vent on roof or wall to allow smoke, cooking smells etc. to escape

machicolation Projecting parapet or ledge on a castle wall whence missiles, boiling water etc. could be dropped on attackers

manor Basic unit of territorial organization in feudal system

monastery House for enclosed order, as opposed to itinerant order, usually in remote areas (e.g. Benedictines)

motte Artificial mound, usually in association with bailey (q.v.) on which the keep was built

neo-classicism Style, based on direct study of Greek and Roman originals, originating *c.* 1750

order The column (base, shaft, capital, entablature) in classical architecture: Doric – simplest and sturdiest form; Corinthian – ornamented with acanthus motif; Ionic – midway between Doric and Corinthian, i.e. more elegant than the former, less decorated than the latter

oriel Bay window

Palladian Of, or pertaining to the Italian architect Andreas Palladio (1518–80). Style introduced into early 17th-century England, revived a century later

pele tower Defensive tower, common in border countries from 13th to 15th centuries

piano nobile Literally 'noble floor'. In Italian palazzi, the first floor, reserved for the family; style later adopted in England

porte cochère Gateway and passage for vehicles through house into courtyard.

piscina Stone basin for water in a church

Pugin, Augustus (1812–52) Architect, ecclesiologist and writer, he believed that Christian religion was expressed only in Gothic art and no other

Repton, Humphrey (1752–1818) Landscape gardener, originally influenced by Capability Brown (q.v.)

Salvin, Anthony (1799–1881) Foremost 19th-century authority on medieval military architecture

screen Wooden, later stone, structure dividing service area of Great Hall from the main area. The *screens passage* (between doors leading into service area and the screen) developed naturally from this

slighting The reduction, partially or wholly, by Parlia-

mentary forces of a Royalist stronghold upon its capture

Smirke, Sir Robert (1781–1867) Architect. Although now best known for his classical work (e.g. the British Museum) his early career embraced the medieval (e.g. Eastnor Castle)

solar Derived from *solarium*. The 'sun room' on the upper floor of a medieval house. Used as family retiring room

Vanbrugh, Sir John (1664–1726) Dramatist and architect. His style was best suited to large-scale buildings, but he also designed a number of smaller houses

vernacular Of, or pertaining to, a region: not cosmopolitan

Verrio, Antonio (1639–1707) Charles II invited him to England to restore the Mortlake tapestries, but his first commission was at Windsor Castle. See also *Laguerre*

BIBLIOGRAPHY

All the houses discussed in this book have individual guides, usually produced by the owners themselves, and usually obtainable only at the house itself. They vary in quality from simple typed sheets to sumptuously produced booklets, but each is unique, providing information on the house not available in general publications and enhancing a visit to the house to an incalculable degree.

Books on the architectural and genealogical history of country houses are legion, ranging from the forelock-tugging accounts of the eighteenth and nineteenth centuries to the monographs published by *Country Life* and *The National Trust* today. An outstanding example is David Green's history of Blenheim Palace in which, drawing on the estate's vast archives, he presents a picture at once detailed and comprehensive of the emergence of a great building. For a general survey, pre-nineteenth century, by two highly intelligent observers see Celia Fiennes' *Journeys* (edited by Christopher Morris, Webb & Bower, 1982) and Daniel Defoe's *Tour through England* (Peter Davies Ltd, reprinted 1927). Indispensable today is *The Country House Guide* by Robin Fedden and John Kenworthy-Brown (Jonathan Cape, 1979) and *The National Trust Guide* (Robin Fedden and Rosemary Joekes, Jonathan Cape, 1979), both mainly architectural but with some social background.

By contrast with architectural and genealogical surveys of country houses, the social life connected with them has been largely ignored until now, a fact which accounts for the success of Mark Girouard's *Life in the English House* (Penguin, 1980). The Duchess of Devonshire's *Chatsworth* (Macmillan, 1982) gives an unusual insight into the running of a great house and also incorporates substantial sections of the sixth Duke's *Handbook*, written in 1844. Two recent books on specific houses – Carol Kennedy's *Harewood* (Hutchinson, 1982) and David Burnett's *Longleat* (Collins, 1978) – place them in the context of today's rapidly changing financial and social conditions. Heather A. Clemenson's *English Country Houses and Landed Estates* (Croom Helm, 1982) is a gallant, single-handed attempt to plot the relationship between the houses and their estates, and show their chances of survival in the late twentieth century.

INDEX

Page numbers in *italic* type indicate illustrations.